THE AGED, THE FAMILY,
AND THE COMMUNITY

The Aged, the Family, and the Community

MINNA FIELD

Columbia University Press
NEW YORK AND LONDON

To all those who aspire
to a happy old age

Copyright © 1972 Columbia University Press
Library of Congress Catalogue Card Number: 79-164500
ISBN: 0-231-03348-6
Printed in the United States of America
10 9 8 7 6 5 4 3 2

FOREWORD

THE THRUST OF THIS PRESENTATION is too often weakened, or even neglected, in the many articles, studies, and discussions of the elderly in our society today. By inference, therefore, the older person is not properly placed in the context of his family but rather considered as an individual who may or may not deserve to be intimately associated with those who comprise the family group in which he should continue as an integral constituent. This undesirable trend is certainly toward separate living arrangements for the several generations. Although there is an increasing number of multigenerational *families* there is a steadily decreasing number of multigenerational *households*.

In these pages the author has described and explained many of the factors which not only produce the so-called "generation gap" but perpetuate it, or at least widen it, beyond the possibility of mutual understanding either of its causes or of the means of lessening it, or doing away with it altogether.

In her description of services to older people, Mrs. Field writes of the "third ear"—the ability to listen to and hear not only what is said, but what is left unsaid, so often the more important and more significant of the two. This vital gift is what the younger generation does not try to achieve or use—and perhaps this may be true to some extent of the older generation as well. But the will should be strong on the part of both to work toward an understanding of what it is that creates avoidable rifts in families and diligently pursue ways of strengthening it as a lasting institution with a kind of cohesiveness which society needs if it is to survive.

The focus on the family as here presented is indeed timely in these unhappy days of turbulence and misunderstanding, and the author deals with it conscientiously for all who are concerned with this aspect of social progress.

OLLIE A. RANDALL

PREFACE

THE 1971 WHITE HOUSE CONFERENCE on Aging concluded its deliberations as this volume went to press.

The recommendations of the conference indicated the need for important government intervention in the future in providing a variety of services essential for improving the conditions under which the elderly of our nation live.

Where do we stand now? How far have we progressed in achieving a "platform and essential action" to improve the status of the elderly? Perhaps a look at the recommendations of the delegates will provide an answer to this question.

The five-day conference (November 28–December 2, 1971) was attended by some 3,500 delegates whose objective was to draft an adequate national policy to meet the pressing needs of the 20,000,000 elderly, especially the more than 8,000,000 who live in poverty. The attitude of the delegates was described as "militant." It was evident from the beginning that they were interested in action rather than discussion. As they put it: "Act. Do not write about us, do not even talk about us, but act."

The conference was divided into fourteen sections, each one of which dealt with a specific area of need and outlined recommendations for meeting the need. The whole embraced every aspect of living which presents difficulties for the older person. In the forefront of their concern were the following topics: (1) income; (2) employment and retirement; (3) roles and activities; (4) physical and mental health needs; (5) housing; (6) nutrition, and (7) transportation.

1. *Income.* The delegates advocated an income floor of $4,500 a year for a couple and 75 percent of that amount for a single person. These amounts would be adjusted from time to time to meet increases in the cost of living, thus assuring an adequate standard of living.

President Nixon, in addressing the conference, stated that he would urge Congress to enact the Welfare Reform bill and changes in Social Security. These would establish a minimum income for the elderly of $130 a month for a single person and $195 for a couple, with provision for automatic adjustments to increases in the cost of living. The President also indicated that he favored a measure to ease the burden of property taxes for the elderly.

The delegates also advocated that no social security retirement benefits be lost if income from earnings is $3,000 a year or less, with a reduction of one dollar in benefits for each two dollars earned beyond $3,000.

2. *Employment and retirement.* Recognizing the importance of continued employment for the elderly, the conference was strongly in favor of abolishing the practice of mandatory retirement and creating a climate of free choice between employment as long as desired by the individual and retirement with an adequate income. This would abolish chronological age as the only criterion for retirement. They also favored workers having a vested interest in pension rights after one year of employment. President Nixon expressed his determination to re-

form private pension systems so that workers may change jobs without losing their pension rights.

3. *Roles and activities.* The provision of satisfying roles and activities, the delegates felt, should be the concern of government, industry, labor, voluntary and religious organizations as well as of the family and the individual involved. They advocated the creation of new role opportunities and preparation for leisure. They felt that families have a responsibility to provide supportive services and that both the old and the young should be involved in programs as they are being formulated.

4. *Physical and mental health needs.* The conference participants urged the merging of medicare and medicaid into one federal system, the elimination of deductibles, and provision for such items as are now not covered, such as drugs, eye and ear care, dental care, care of the feet, and such supplies as these demanded. Adequate care and outreach services were seen as alternatives to institutionalization. It was also pointed out that the conference favored extension of such services to the total population under a national health plan. President Nixon pledged the funding of a variety of aid programs for specific services, such as home care. He promised to increase the appropriation for the Administration on Aging to $100 million for such state and local services as home health aids, homemaker services, and so forth.

5. *Housing.* The conferees declared that a national policy on housing is imperative. They advocated the provision of 120,000 units a year for the elderly, to be financed by the federal, state, and local governments. Such housing would provide not only shelter, but also such services as may be needed to encourage independent living in confort and dignity, thus avoiding the need for institutionalization in may instances.

6. *Nutrition.* The delegates urged the development of a program of rehabilitation of the malnourished elderly as well as a preventive program of adequate nutrition for those who are approaching old age. They suggested the expansion of the programs of prepared meals for the elderly and utilization of high school cafeterias for that purpose. Food stamps, they said, should be made more generously available to meet the escalation in the cost of living. President Nixon stated that the additional funds to state and localities, previously discussed, could be utilized for the prepared meals programs.

7. *Transportation.* An increase in transportation facilities in both urban and rural communities was seen as one of the priorities, drawing attention to a problem which has grown considerably since the previous conference held ten years ago. The delegates advocated a reduction or elimination of fares for older people. They also stressed the need for volunteer drivers where public transportation is not available, or where the elderly are not able to avail themselves of public transportation.

The delegates were also concerned with a number of all-embracing aspects of life. Among these were the necessity of re-ordering the nation's priorities; the appointment of an ombudsman; the reorganization of the Administration on Aging to make it an effective advocate agency; and the establishment of a Center for Aging in the National Institute of Mental Health.

It was recognized that some of the goals advocated by the delegates could not be realized in the immediate future since time would be required for legislative action to be taken in some instances and funds for cash benefits to be made available in others. Nevertheless, the discussion of these issues and the feeling of urgency which was apparent in the sessions, it was felt, could not help but create more favorable conditions.

I am deeply grateful to Miss Ollie A. Randall, Principal Consultant on Aging, Ford Foundation, for reading the first draft of the manuscript, for making her helpful comments, and for writing the Foreword.

My thanks to Dr. E. M. Bluestone, former Director of Montefiore Hospital, New York, for his encouragement and support.

A debt of gratitude is due to the social agencies, hospitals, and schools of social work—too numerous to mention here—for sharing their knowledge of the problems of the elderly and for allowing me to consult their case records.

Most of all, I am indebted to the many elderly people who gave me a firsthand account of what aging means to them and a deeper appreciation than I could obtain in any other way of the deprivations which our society often imposes on the older generation.

MINNA FIELD

CONTENTS

THE AGED, THE FAMILY,
AND THE COMMUNITY

1. INTRODUCTION

HISTORIANS WILL NOTE that within the past few decades there has been discernible evidence of an increased concern with the status of the elderly, and an awareness of the importance of the numerous and manifold problems which are precipitated by the aging process. This is in striking contrast to the casual and indifferent attitudes of the past when the plight of the elderly was too often regarded as the result of a lack of foresight, or of an ill-spent youth. Such help as the elderly needed, was felt to be the sole responsibility of their former dependents. Too often, however, children failed to assume this responsibility despite the fact that, as a moral attitude, disregard of the parents was in conflict with the Ten Commandments. And so the geriatric problem multiplied and deepened with the increase of the elderly in our midst.

A more humane attitude in the form of a more productive interest is beginning to take shape. This embraces a greater sensitivity to the numerous privations which the elderly almost always experience, sooner or later, as well as a growing responsiveness to the unhappiness which these conditions generate for the older person and for those closely associated with him. It is being more widely recognized that the older person cannot, in most instances, be held responsible for the inescapable difficulties which the advancing years impose on him. Nor are family members always in a position to meet the various needs of their elderly relatives.

The mounting numbers of older people and the lengthened life expectancy have stimulated appreciation of the fact that old age is one of the most pressing medical-social problems of our time. The emergence of this improved understanding is leading us to a deepening responsibility for the establishment of important and far-reaching measures and remedies designed at least to cushion the impact of the more severe manifestations of age. More attention is now being paid to the social and economic insecurity of the aged, to the poor response of society to it; to the hazards and consequences of failing health and to the unavailability of essential facilities for health and medical care; to the difficulty in finding and establishing living quarters which can maintain integrity and self-respect for as long as possible, and to the lack of opportunities for the fruitful utilization of free time.

To meet the deleterious effects of prevailing deficiencies, more attention is being devoted to the study of the problems and to the appropriate measures required for their solution. We have seen the passage of the Social Security Act designed to improve income maintenance; of Medicare and Medicaid aimed at providing more satisfactory medical care than had hitherto been available; experimental ventures in the construction of housing which take into consideration the needs of the elderly as well as the handicaps which old age often brings; the establishment and expansion of community centers under various auspices which offer educational and recreational activities to meet the needs of these participants and encourage socialization among them. All these services and facilities, under whatever auspices they are established, show a growing concern with the need to create a favorable milieu in which the elderly can achieve a greater sense of fulfillment and dignity.

Some new steps, such as the appointment in 1969 of a United States Commissioner on Aging and the 1971 White House Conference on Aging which drew attention to the changes needed in all areas of living, are hopeful signs of intensifying action (results will not be known until 1972).

Important as these developments are, they still fall short of a total answer to the unhappiness and discouragement which too often afflict the elderly. It is now becoming recognized that, in addition to being distressed by the lack of proper facilities, the elderly are disturbed by their alienation from the life around them, and especially so by their unsatisfactory relationship with, or even estrangement from, the younger generations.

Books, articles in professional and popular periodicals, as well as the news media, are more and more drawing attention to the strained family relationships which exist between the older and the younger generations, and to their injurious effects on the older individuals. In fact, the expression "generation gap" which is used as a kind of euphemism to designate friction between parents and children has become a household word, and like most such expressions, it covers a multitude of sins. The slightest disagreement is considered a manifestation of the generation gap, carrying with it the implication of an irreconcilable and irremediable rift.

Interest in, and concern for, this latter-day way of life in family relationships is understandable. The family unit has long been regarded as the cornerstone of our social structure. The need and importance of cementing it have been consistently preached, if not practiced. The designation "family unit," however, is applied nowadays only to the so-called "nuclear family"—the family of parents and dependent children. The moment the older person reaches what is considered arbitrarily to be "old age," and even earlier when he no longer resides with his married children, he ceases to be regarded as a family member in the traditional sense and is unjustly excluded from the family unit. The fact that the older person, even when he no longer shares the home, nevertheless remains parent to one or more of the adult members of the nuclear family, and grandparent to the children, is too often disregarded and neglected.

Such extrusion of the elderly from the life of the family group and its unwholesome effects cannot be dismissed lightly. If one shares the conviction that the older person is and must remain a member of the family group, regardless of his age or infirmities (and perhaps in spite of them), then one must look searchingly into the underlying reasons for the alienation of the elderly. Amelioration of the deteriorating relationship between the generations is a matter of vital concern to all ages (and particularly to the young, who look forward to a happy old age) if we are to achieve and maintain better living conditions for all of them.

What are the factors responsible for our failure to solve this important and disturbing problem? The question which cries out for a solution is whether there is a direct or indirect cause-and-effect relationship between the various difficulties which impinge on the individual as he ages and the relationship that actually exists between the older and the younger generations.

If we are to find an answer to this question, we must reexamine and update our knowledge and understanding of what it means to grow old; the nature and extent of the difficulties and hardships which are encountered in the process of aging; the older as well as the younger person's reaction to them; and their long-range effect on all family members. We must know what can be done to help the elderly to achieve a more tolerable old age, what steps have already been taken to that end, and what still remains to be done.

We will address ourselves to such questions in the pages that follow. This involves, first of all, a determination of the circumstances which create hardships for the older person. How important is the role played by the tempo of change in our society? What is the effect of unfavorable moral, political, and economic conditions, of deteriorating physical and mental health, of poor living arrangements, and of unproductive free time?

We will seek to answer such questions as: (1) What effect do such hardships as prevailing conditions create, have on the older person's self-image and self-respect? (2) How do they affect his relationship with his children? (3) What is the adult children's reaction as they are confronted with the implications of these difficulties? (4) How can this relationship be improved? And finally (5) What is the role of the social worker when faced with a breakdown in family relationships? What contribution can the social worker make to soften the harsh effects of broken family relationships of this kind?

Theoretical discussion will not monopolize these pages. It will be supplemented practically by case records from agencies which deal extensively with the everyday problems confronting the elderly in their struggle for continued effective survival. It will also be based on interviews with administrators of homes for the aged and of senior-citizen centers in all their variety, as well as on the author's personal experience with elderly individuals, in order to secure firsthand reactions to their uncertain status in society and to the shift in authority within families which transfers dominion to younger hands.

There will also be a discussion of basic philosophical principles which govern social work practice, and an examination of prevailing trends. These exert an important influence on the services available (or not available) to ameliorate the severity of the geriatric phenomenon.

2. *WHO ARE THE AGED?*

BEFORE WE CAN ATTEMPT any discussion of the problems of the elderly, their effects on all of us, the reactions which they call forth in families, friends, and neighbors, and the effect of such reactions on all environmental relationships, we must be clear on what we mean by the term "aged." When does *old* age begin? How many aged are there in the community, and what is their proportion in the total population? What are the trends which portend an increase or a decrease in the number of aged in the near future? Answers to these questions will influence the severity of the pressure with which we are confronted and to which we will have to respond.

When Does Old Age Begin?

The understanding of what constitutes old age varies in different cultures and at different times. In a very real sense it reveals the measure of our civilization. Suffice it to say that in all primitive societies, and in some which are not so primitive, where the life span is short, our "middle age" is their "old age." In our own society the designation of old age depends to a large extent on the age of the person discussing it. The young, for example, tend to consider every adult as "old." Nor does the term "old" indicate whether we are interpreting it chronologically, physiologically, psychologically or socially.

We do not, as yet, have a clear definition of "old." We know in a vague way that old age is something which we must face in the hazy future. The question as to who is "aged" was settled for us politically when the Social Security Administration arbitrarily decided that retirement age and eligibility for benefits under the new Social Security Act would begin at age 65 (later amended to 62), thus equating retirement age with old age. In doing so, we took as our guide the example set in Germany where Chancellor Bismarck introduced social security provisions in old age, at a time when few people reached an age we now consider "old."

Following the pattern set many years ago, however, fails to take into consideration the fact that the situation is very different in our country today from what it was in Germany at that time. Here, the number of persons 65 years of age and over represents about one tenth of the entire population and, according to the Social Security Administration, there are more than three thousand individuals in the United States over 100 years old who are receiving benefits.

Despite these different conditions, the concept of 65 as defining retirement and therefore "old age" has become all-pervasive, so much a part of our thinking that we often classify and speak of the elderly as "the 65 and over," or "the 65-plus," without any thought of the fact that in so doing we reduce all elderly people, the able-bodied and sound of mind as well as the disabled and incapacitated, to an indiscriminate mass. The result is a lack of analysis of the human variations among them and of their surviving potentials. This, in turn, affects our planning for the elderly.

This prevailing attitude raises a number of pertinent questions. Let us now consider some of the implications of defining old age so closely in relation to eligibility for social security benefits.

It is confidently predicted, for instance, that social security benefits will be conferred at earlier ages in the future. Does this mean that the aging period will lengthen to keep pace with the changes in the eligibility requirements of the social security system? For that matter, should we stamp as "aged" those who are 62 years old since both men and women are now eligible for social security benefits at that age? Or, does it mean that the designation "old" will in the future change with whatever changes occur in the social security system?

At what age shall we identify the aged? We find frequent references to people over 55 as being euphemistically called "senior citizens." How far are we from the day when those over 45 will be so considered, as they are now already considered too old for employment?

Even accepting current definitions of old age, can we believe that anyone who is 62 or 65 is in the same age group, that he is confronted with the same needs, and requires the same facilities to meet these needs, as those who are 80 or 90 years old?

The arbitrariness of the accepted definition was underlined in a paper delivered in 1968 at the 21st Annual University of Michigan Conference when a representative of the Administration on Aging of the U.S. Department of Health, Education, and Welfare, while trying to define the aged, took as his guide the group 75 years of age and over! He frankly admitted that his dividing line was arbitrary but that he accepted it as being more suitable for his purposes. He added that anyone can similarly choose his own dividing line.

As we look at the problem, it becomes clear that there is no fixed age at which one suddenly becomes old. It is a gradual process. Some hold that aging starts from birth. We now find reference in the literature to the "younger old," those under 75, and the "older old," those over 75. These labels are, of course, arbitrary and cannot apply to all the people on one or the other side of the line.

Despite existing differences, and despite the arbitrary definition of 65 as "old age," the fact remains that the line drawn by the Social Security Act has an important bearing on many aspects of the older person's life. Thus, for want of greater flexibility and making allowances for the automatic, physiological, and pathological differences—physical and mental—we will accept for our discussion the prevailing concept of 65 as the figure at which old age begins, and which thus tentatively serves as a line of demarcation between the older and the younger generations.

Number of Elderly and Rate of Increase

How many aged people are there in our society and what is their proportion in the total population? Is the number of elderly stationary, increasing, or decreasing? To answer these questions one needs only consult the census figures and the information contained in the Periodic Population Reports of the U.S. Government, which show that the number of aged in the nation is large and that the rate of increase in relation to the rest of the population, as well as in absolute numbers, is considerable.

As far back as 1934 it was stated that in "two generations [since 1850] the number of persons over 65 years of age increased from less than 600,000 to over 6,500,000, or eleven times, while the population has increased only five times." [1] This proportion of increase in the number of the elderly in relation to the increase of the population as a whole has continued since that time. Thus we find that, according to figures issued by the U.S. Department of Health, Education, and Welfare in 1968, "during the past 68 years this group [the aged] increased seven times its former size, while the population as a whole grew to three times its former size." [2]

At the beginning of the twentieth century, there were some three million people over 65 years of age. This number doubled in 1930 and had increased five times by 1965 to some fifteen million persons. In 1968, the elderly numbered eighteen million and, according to the latest U.S. Census (1970), those aged 65 and over numbered 20,049,592 in 1970.[3] It is predicted that in the next twenty years the older population of the United States will reach twenty-five to thirty million. It is reasonable to assume that, as was the case with predictions in the past, this may well prove to be an underestimate.

It is important to keep in mind that, with the life span now extending to 100 years or even more in some cases, the the aged do not fall into one age group. In fact, almost one third are 75 years of age or older. As compared with those who are now in the 65-year-old group, they differ not only in the severity of the deficiencies which their more advanced age imposes, but also in their ability to cope with such deficiencies; as a result, they require different services to meet their essential needs.

[1] Rubinow, *Quest for Security*, p. 224.
[2] Brotman, "Every Tenth American," p. 3.
[3] U.S. Census of Population Report, p. 4 Table II.

Early Manifestation of Interest

Older people were always an inescapable segment of our society, regardless of the age at which they were considered to be "old." As indicated by the statistics, the number of elderly at the beginning of the century was small. As they reached a more advanced age, their decreased physical strength, illnesses, and disabilities made it impossible for them to meet their needs unaided. However, so long as their number was small, and so long as they lived in tightly knit families and communities, their need for help was met, as a matter of course, by members of their immediate family, their friends, and neighbors. Their religion helped in a practical as well as a spiritual way. Their plight passed almost unnoticed by society at large. When their infirmities increased this kind of help became unavailable or inadequate, the last resort open to them was the dreaded poorhouse at the entrance of which they left all hope behind.

But changing vital statistics brought their own pressures for more insight and change. Medical advances, by decreasing mortality rates, especially in the early years, through the conquest of the infectious and contagious diseases, increased average life expectancy and enabled more people to survive to old age. The lengthened life span for the newborn thus achieved, changed the age distibution of the population, raising the proportion of the elderly perceptibly. The impact of the number of elderly and their concentration in urban areas could not help but draw the attention of society to the problems confronting these people residing in their midst. This led to a greater sense of responsibility, producing new remedies for emerging problems.

At first, such interest and responsibility were manifested primarily by church groups and fraternal organizations. Organized charity was slow to recognize and respond to the needs of this particular section of the population. This lack of sensitivity to the misery of the old persisted into the twentieth century. We find, for instance, that in 1908 the opinion was expressed at the National Conference of Charities and Corrections that the "agitation for State Pensions [for the aged] in the United States is ill-advised, in that the problem of poverty in old age, as generally met with, is primarily the result of ill-spent years, or ill-spent earnings, or ill-spent savings." [4] This would seem to indicate that there was little appreciation of the economic difficulties in which the elderly found themselves. These difficulties may have been, and usually were, due to circumstances beyond their control, such as poor economic conditions, low wages, the expense of raising a growing family, or the possibility that illness or other emergencies may have interfered with their ability to provide for the later years. Poverty may have been a social illness which was more than its victims could prevent.

There came a time, however, when the help which eventually became available from organized philanthropy was insufficient to cope with the variety and severity of the problems afflicting the ever growing number of older people. Slowly the conviction grew that the only solution to these problems was to be found in some form of governmental intervention. Assistance to the elderly under government auspices was long practiced by various countries in Europe and other parts of

[4] Hoffman, p. 229.

the world. In Denmark, for instance, it has been in effect since 1891. The United States, however, adhering to its emphasis on rugged individualism plus voluntary effort, was slow to respond to the need for assistance through governmental action.

There were, of course, the lonely voices of such farsighted individuals as the late Dr. I. M. Rubinow, a pioneer in the movement for social insurance in the United States, who early recognized the tragedy and helplessness of the old person faced with overwhelming odds. As far back as 1916, he advocated adequate provisions for the care of the elderly, devoting a chapter in his book *Social Insurance* to what he called "The Old Man's Problem." Despite his advocacy, however, and the efforts of Abraham Epstein, the founder and guiding spirit of the American Association for Old Age Security, and numerous books and articles devoted to this subject, many years passed before action was taken to establish the program of care which these pioneers outlined.

It took the depression of the 1930s, which further aggravated the plight of the elderly by draining the resources of those who were previously in a position to come to their aid, as well as their own resources, to stimulate a more systematic plan of assistance. The first step in that direction was taken by the government in 1930, in the form of public assistance to needy individuals over 70 years of age. Though the provisions of that act left much to be desired, it did render invaluable service by reestablishing the obligation of government to step in when its dependent people would otherwise be helpless.

This first step was followed in succeeding years by two separately enacted measures—Old Age Relief and Old Age Assistance. Both these measures were far from adequate. They not only failed to meet basic needs, they were weighed down by a variety of restrictions, such as residence requirements and the imposition of a "means test," which failed to eliminate the stigma of "charity." Their most undesirable feature was the enforcement of responsibility for the support of their elders by children and even grandchildren, frequently through court action. This enforcement imposed severe hardships on members of the family as well as on the older person himself. After many years, intercession by socially minded individuals and social work organizations, familiar at firsthand with the detrimental results of this hardship, succeeded in abolishing this requirement of the law.

Despite all their inadequacies these early measures were instrumental in paving the way for the next step in the government's assumption of its responsibility to care for the aged, namely, passage of the Social Security, Medicare, and Medicaid acts. Details of these programs, their benefits and inadequacies, as well as their influence on the position of the elderly, will be discussed later in this volume.

Important as governmental subsidy and support can be in helping with the problems of the elderly, they cannot altogether resolve difficulties in the area of intrafamilial relationships. Such relationships are personal and cannot be legislated. Neither can family disharmony be achieved by a building program of adequate housing for the elderly, nor by the establishment of specialized facilities designed to fill the vacuum of empty days. All such remedies can, however, contribute to the reduction of pressures, tensions, and strains, and in this way they can help to reduce friction generated by the interaction of youth and age. If we are to dig down to the roots of the intergenerational clash which we see all too often, we must address ourselves to an understanding of the factors which underlie it and come to grips with them.

3. THE IMPACT OF SOCIAL CHANGES ON THE GENERATIONS

THIS CENTURY HAS SHOWN significant changes in the status of the elderly, and these can be ascribed to many factors. Foremost among them is the structure of society which determines the background conditions and social climate in which the elderly must live out their years. It has serious implications for all the generations, and for the welfare of the older person in particular, exerting a profound influence on such alternatives as coexistence, confrontation, and total estrangement.

No one will dispute the fact that as the years go by, they will sooner or later affect adversely the position of the older person and exercise a strong impact on his sense of personal dignity. As a result, we find that as a senior citizen the older person loses status and is subjected to isolation, segregation, and many other deprivations which are inflicted on him as a member of a minority group, in the same way as other minority groups have been since time immemorial treated by the rest of society. Unfortunately, age is a crippling handicap which those who surround the elderly rather than he himself must strive to overcome.

What are the changes in our society which bring about the change in attitude toward the older person?

Changes in Social Structure

Until the middle of the nineteenth century, the United States was predominantly a rural, agricultural society. The family was a cohesive unit, living in close proximity, engaged in a common effort, and having common interests. Within this culture, the older members had an important role to play, being regarded by the younger generation as teachers and counselors who had grown old in wisdom and practical knowledge of living. Accumulated experience and skills, acquired in the course of a lifetime, were vital since they made a substantial contribution to the advancement of their families and of the community as a whole. It was accepted as a matter of course that the younger generation would continue to live in the community while caring for the ancestral farm. Even when the older person was no longer able to produce physically, his value to the family was not diminished since he was looked up to for mature advice and guidance. The care of the older person was considered to be a normal responsibility of the family, and he shared the family home as long as he lived.

With the advent of the Industrial Revolution came the shift from an agricultural to an industrial society. This was accompanied by successive waves of migration and transplantation from the rural to the urban community, changing the structure of society as well as the basic conditions of life for both the old and the young. A great deal has been written about the mobility of American society, particularly of this time. Studies indicate that "about nine of every ten persons one year old and over in the United States in April 1959 moved at least once in their lifetime," and that "of the population 18 years old and over, only 1.5 percent always lived in the same house." [1]

EFFECT ON THE YOUNGER GENERATION

As the young adult left the farm to move into the city and became part of the industrial society, he found new activities, new interests, and new friends within a more complicated social pattern than he had known before. These new interests and the newly acquired financial independence of the young industrial worker combined to widen the gap between the young adult and his parents.

In the rural society, the family home was the center of daily living, and a close relationship existed not only between parents and children, but also among all members of the related family group—grandparents, uncles, aunts, and cousins, all of them interested in, and concerned with, the welfare of the others. This tight circle tended to lose its significance and influence when the young adult left the family home and moved to the industrialized center. Family ties began to weaken and, in time, became more or less severed. Even where contact could be maintained, it was likely to be confined to casual, widely spaced visits for family gatherings on special occasions.

EFFECT ON THE ELDERLY

What is the effect on the elderly person when the young who surround him leave the family home to take their place in the expanding industrial society and in the more exciting life of the urban centers?

[1] *Mobility of the Population of the United States, April, 1958, to 1959*, p. 1.

Frequently, the older person, left to shift for himself, with such help as his wife might give, found himself unable to cope unaided with the essentials of farm work. Under these circumstances, the farm was often absorbed by more aggressive farmers who possessed modern machinery and could operate larger tracts of land more efficiently and more productively. Finding it more difficult to earn a living, the small farmer may have had to seek the help of friends, and relatives, or the public agency for the satisfaction of his everyday personal needs. And so we find that the elderly individual, unable to provide for himself, and in order to remove himself from this unhappy situation, often decided to move to the city. It has been said that it is not so much the affluence of the city as the poverty of the farm that is responsible for the migration of large numbers of older persons to the cities. Often the decision to move was reinforced by the hope that things would improve when he moved closer to his children.

Unfortunately, this attempt at a solution of the family problem rarely succeeds. The discovery is made that the comparatively small city apartment is inadequate to accommodate additional people, even assuming that the generations would want to live together, which is not always the case.

Furthermore, the mobility of the population is not confined to movement from the rural to the urban community. The young adult may be obliged to transfer from one city to another as a result, for example, of the practice of corporations to shift their employees about in an effort to employ their skills to the utmost. The elderly person who had moved to the city in order to be near his children often finds it difficult, or even impossible, to reintegrate with them. Distance tends to erode close family relationships by removing the beneficial effects of intimate day-to-day associations.

Having been uprooted from his accustomed surroundings

in his hopeful efforts at wholesome relocation, floundering in the unfamiliar urban environment, and deprived of the support of those close to him, the older person is furthermore subjected to various destructive and debilitating pressures. Crowded living conditions, noise, unavoidable association with disinterested strangers, higher living costs—all are strange and frightening to him.

In this unaccustomed environment, he is thrown on his own inadequate resources, and finds little opportunity to utilize skills learned and developed over a lifetime. He is thus able to participate in neither the industrial nor the social life of the community while at the same time he is deprived of the warmth and concern of those who should be closest to him. He is disturbed by the growing alienation from his children and, unable to provide for himself, he may often find it necessary to turn to strangers for help. It is to be expected, under these circumstances, that the older man will suffer from the number and complexity of the problems confronting him.

The difference in the provisions made for the care of the elderly, as these are influenced by the nature of the society in which they live—whether the environment is urban or rural—is clearly illustrated if we compare the Amish and Mennonites of the Pennsylvania Dutch country.

Though both groups live within the same geographical area, their social structures differ. The Amish remain a farming people with close family ties. It is taken for granted that the family farm will be inherited and maintained by the children; that the family group will remain intact; and that so long as the parents live they will continue to be part of the children's household—if necessary, an addition will be built to the children's home to accomodate their parents. This arrangement is adhered to even when the parents are no longer productive.

Seldom do any of the Amish elderly enter a home for the aged so long as there is a surviving family member to care for them.

The Mennonites, on the other hand, are not an agricultural people. They do not have the large farmhouses of the Amish, where the old parents can eventually be accommodated. The community is acutely conscious of, and emphasizes its concern for, the welfare of the elderly by pointing to the many adequate homes for the aged provided for the older people. This arrangement, they maintain, is accepted by both the old and the young as a normal and even a desirable way of life.

Effect of Extended Periods of Education

The increased mobility of the population resulting from changes in our economic structure is not the only factor that influences adversely the maintenance of close family ties and, consequently, the stability of family relationships. Some of the estrangement is due also to the alleged need to provide the younger generation with an extended period of education. This is prompted by our increased appreciation of the advantages of an education, as well as by the fact that it enables the young people to compete more effectively in meeting the demands of industry, a fact which is reinforced by the parents' ambition for their children "to get ahead."

The achievement of this goal involves expensive attendance at college over several years, frequently at a considerable distance from home. In the past, a college education was taken for granted by a comparatively small group of young people and subsidized for the large part by their elders. When college attendance necessitated leaving the parental home, it was considered by both the student and his parents as an unavoidable but temporary separation.

Nowadays, the ambition to have a college education is characteristic of a larger number of young people, frequently involving a financial sacrifice on the part of hard-working parents. Furthermore, both the older and the younger generations seem to proceed on the assumption that attendance at a college away from home, even when there is one available nearby, is somehow conducive to what is being referred to as a "more rounded education."

As a result of the long separation which attendance at a college away from home requires, the young person becomes quite accustomed to the freedom of an independent existence in a less restrictive environment away from his parents, and usually prefers to establish a home of his own upon graduation. In achieving this goal, he is helped by the fact that, being well equipped educationally, he is able to secure an adequate-paying position, and is thus able to maintain an independent establishment. The temporary separation becomes an irreversible one, and the parental home is no longer a place of residence, but rather a place to visit on occasion. This separation has profound implications for both generations.

The desire of the young unmarried adult (particularly the young woman) to move away from the parental home was viewed in the past by the parents with apprehension. For one thing, it was a serious break with tradition. In addition, the parents found it difficult to understand why their son or daughter should be attracted away from their home, or even be repulsed by it. They felt that their children had everything provided for them and failed to see why they preferred to settle in a small apartment where living was often at a lower standard than the one which they were accustomed to enjoy. The parents were naturally hurt by the threatening cleavage between themselves and their children and wondered wherein they had failed. By contrast, the move today is generally accepted almost as a matter of course. In fact, for a grown man or woman to remain in the parental home is often considered almost unnatural and not in the best interests of the self-confident young.

The net result of this separation is that contact between the parents and their mature children is confined to such occasional visits as distance and other diverting interests permit. The emphasis on priorities shifts from the old to the young. As the years pass, there develops a break in the continuity of interests, communication becomes limited to trivialities, resulting in a loss of a significant exchange on matters which may be of genuine concern to both sides. The young, caught up in the new world of technological miracles, frequently regard their parents as living in the past, poorly informed, and having little understanding of the new trends and fashions. In other words, there develops an ill-founded feeling that the old folks are, *ipso facto*, "Old-fashioned." Physical separation thus too often leads to a spiritual and emotional separation. The generations become progressively estranged, and there develops what is often referred to by our latter-day psychologists as a "failure of communication."

As day-to-day contacts diminish, the younger generation, as well as the older one, accepts the "facts of life," as they call them. This, they maintain, is the normal way. The parents feel, even if they may not say so (and when they do, apologetically), that the "young have a right to a life of their own." So far as the grown children are concerned, they look upon the older person as someone who, by virtue of his age, restricts this right. To the surprise of few, this negative attitude leads in many instances to the unfulfillment of responsibililty for the involvement of youth with the parental problems of age.

Emphasis on Youth and Productivity

One of the less desirable products of a good education is the self-denying partiality to youth on the part of the older generation, of which the cover-all sentiment that the young "have a right to a life of their own" is but one manifestation. But, while conceding the "right," we can question its logic and its exclusiveness. In the end, we shall have to decide the degree of deprivation suffered by both sides in relation to each other, and the benefits reasonably to be expected from any decision.

The existing accent on youth is a product of our historical beginnings. During the early period of our country's expansion, there was a compelling need for a young and strong population to meet the challenge of conquering, defending, and settling a large undeveloped territory. This concept of the overriding importance of youthful vigor and courage continues to dominate the process of evolution in American society. No serious question is being raised as to whether this vital quality continues to be as important under present conditions as it was in the past.

The survival of this attitude and the explanation that the United States is still a young country continue to promote the priority of youth, frequently blinding us to the potentialities of the older generation. As a result, aging comes to be regarded as a somewhat hopeless state, while its hopeful advantages are disregarded. Little or no attention is paid to the positive values of maturity, experience, knowledge, and wisdom, which many of those who attain old age can and often do exhibit if they are given the opportunity, and if they are not "senile" in the medical sense of this term.

It is interesting to contrast this attitude with the one prevailing in the distant land of Hunza where, it is reported, men sometimes attain the unbelievable age of 145, and where

the attitude toward old age is a healthy one. These centenarians are encouraged to teach and train their juniors in their particular arts and skills. They are needed in the community and are not set aside. There is no time or place for the depression of futility, frustration, or idleness, such as our civilization encourages.[2]

This description of the way the elderly are treated in far-off and primitive Hunza is reminiscent of our own attitudes in earlier days.

The Generation Gap

The so-called "generation gap" is sometimes referred to in a negative way as "the intergenerational conflict." These terms may be comparatively new in common parlance, but the problem they connote is old. There appears always to have been difficulty in communication between the generations, to which some of the injunctions in Scripture and other religious documents refer, directly or indirectly. We often find references in the literature to such difficulties in the "good old days." There is evidence to show that in the earliest times the young complained of parents who "do not understand them." Perhaps nature can explain such phenomena, though it does not teach us how to deal with them.

In our own time, we are more and more aware of the widen-

[2] Beck and Stangle, p. 118.

ing gap in mores, values, and beliefs. There may, of course, be unavoidable, often irreconcilable, differences between the generations under unfavorable circumstances. Such differences are the result of changes in outlook, in religious thinking (or lack of it), in what we may still refer to with some nostalgia as respect for age—all part of the intellectual ideas accompanying technological advances and the inability of youth to see the potentialities of the older person as these apply to the new order of things. Whatever the reason, it appears that the young who rejoice in their health and strength have little sympathy for those whose health and strength have vanished.

The gap is further widened by a new attitude among the young which exhibits overt hostility and lack of confidence (as shown in the expression "you cannot trust anyone over thirty"). It is this careless and often callous attitude which makes the generation gap such a negative and damaging force in family relationships.

Whether this latter-day attitude stems from a mindless rebellion against what is referred to unintelligibly as the "establishment," or whether it has its roots in childhood conflicts with parental authority (as the reference to "over thirty" would seem to imply), it does not stop at the tender age of rebellious youth. All too often, the same attitude is carried over into the relationship of grown children to their elders. In any event, it must be held responsible for the isolation of the old and their exclusion from the protective umbrella of the integrated family. Some have jumped to the conclusion that this separation of the elderly is the automatic result of their voluntary withdrawal from society. One cannot help questioning its voluntariness. Rather, it may be, and almost always is, an enforced reaction of the elderly as they sense their rejection by the young. It is often the older persons' meekness, their humility, which determines their role in such a relationship. In either case, it results in an alienation which is destructive of the older person's rights and privileges.

One must agree with Dr. E. M. Bluestone that "age presents characteristics and requirements which differ sufficiently from those of youth to justify our concern, and more so because, by all the signs, they influence the unity, the integrity, and the stability of the family, for better or for worse." [3] Knowing these prevailing differences, it becomes the responsibility of all, professionals and nonprofessionals, to safeguard the traditional rights of the elderly within the family group, and to do all in their power to stem the unfriendly tide and achieve a greater tolerance for the "underdog," so to speak, in our midst. When all is said and done, the strong must protect the weak. This is best accomplished by close proximity and certainly not by excessive distance.

EFFECT OF THESE CHANGES ON FAMILY RELATIONSHIPS

In view of all the difficulties which are inherent in the concept of age (and these are built in by nature from birth), the achievement in practice of such an understanding and tolerance is seldom an easy matter. Whatever may be the explanation for these difficulties—whether it lies in the mobility of the population, the effects of early separation, or society's partiality to youth and its productivity—they combine to have an important bearing on the status of the older person, on his self-confidence and self-esteem, and on the relationship which binds him to his children.

Even when the older person understands the reasons for the various degrees of estrangement, it does not follow that he

[3] Bluestone, "The Growing Impact of Longer Years on Society—a Salute to Youth and a Plea," p. 31.

can accept them easily. Added to all the other hardships which beset him, and perhaps the hardest to overcome, is the glorification of youth by our society in all of its aspects because of its strength, its vitality, its physical attractiveness, and its promise (for everything but its own old age). These attitudes confer benefits on the young at the expense of age and are unjust to this extent.

We frequently see the older person, in a supreme effort to overcome such barriers to a more wholesome relationship, struggling against odds and at personal cost to find ready substitutes for these highly prized qualities, no matter how impossible such a task may appear to be. Those who are old have certain commonly accepted characteristics which mark them as old. Says Dr. Robert Kastenbaum:

The elderly person is marked in more ways than one. His face, hands, and all those body parts which are significant in social communication have become unmistakably engraved with age. Before he speaks he has already identified himself to others as a person who occupies an extreme position in the spectrum of life. Should his words and actions also betray those features we associate with advanced age, then we are further encouraged to mark him down as one who is strikingly different from ourselves.[4]

We have thus far been emphasizing the negative aspects of the relationship between the older and the younger generations. It must be kept in mind, however, that their difficulties do not apply uniformly to all of the elderly. There are many families in which the ties binding the generations remain close and warm, where distance, when it must be imposed, does not serve as an impassable barrier to a satisfying relationship, and where the adult children show an unflagging concern for their elders, and a readiness to assume the burden of help uncomplainingly when such help is required.

[4] Kastenbaum, "The Foreshortened Life Perspective," p. 126.

The subject of these remarks is that segment of the older population—and it is unfortunately a large segment indeed—which is deprived of familial interest and support, whose children have become estranged (it is seldom the other way round), sometimes through circumstances beyond their control, at other times because of unresolved, perhaps vindictive, attitudes carried over from a resentful childhood.

It is in these and similar situations that the older person is left to shift for himself and to face unaided the plight of later years, at a time when he can bear it least, when he is compelled, for self-preservation, to seek comfort and help from strangers. Under these circumstances, the elderly person must attempt to make a difficult, and often unattainable, adjustment. Adjustments confront us in the course of a total lifetime, but we must concede that they are particularly difficult for the man in the later years of life. When he was young, there was always anticipation of something better. The older man is deprived of hope as he faces the cheerless prospect of lonely incapacity.

It is to combat these feelings of estrangement, uselessness, loneliness, and depression that the old person needs evidence of warmth, concern, and a reasonable amount of stimulation from the younger members of his family. These are the qualities of the blood relationship of which he is so frequently deprived.

Another factor which disturbs the elderly person is that he has been removed from productive employment and the interest as well as social contacts which such employment provided over a lifetime. He may attempt to compensate for this loss by wishing to share the interests of his children and derive satisfaction from their accomplishments. Unfortunately, the younger generation, excited by new developments in which they have the opportunity to participate, too often fail to share new and stimulating experiences with their parents, perhaps fearing that parental brakes thoughtlessly applied might cramp their style. They seem to justify such failures by assuming that their parents, whose education and experience may have been different from their own, might be unable to understand the importance of their own involvement. What they overlook in their tendency to jump to conclusions is the importance to the old man of hearing about the new developments, so that he can derive a vicarious satisfaction and perhaps a sense of participation. The knowledge that his children want to share their experiences with him is an important part of the state of coexistence.

The breakdown in mutual understanding which results from the children's frequent withdrawal into a world strictly their own—the distance between the generations which is a response to the mobility of the population; the increasing role of the machine in many aspects of living and the concomitant devaluation of the "human machine"—has created breaches in the fabric of family solidarity. Some misguided observers are convinced that the traditional family as a protective institution may no longer be necessary and is, in fact, on the wane. Others, however, are equally sure that human beings will continue to have emotional and psychological needs which will have particular significance in the later years of life. They hold that satisfaction of these needs can be assured only through wholesome interaction within the family group.

Those who are convinced of the importance of the satisfaction of these emotional needs and are faced with the threat inherent in the loosening of family ties must devise ways and means to preserve and strengthen the positive values inherent in family life. Children tend to carry over into their own relationship with their parents that which they have observed in the behavior of their parents to their grandparents. This suggests the possibility of utilizing constructively the three-generation family, and the importance of preserving worthwhile traditions with such adjustments as life may compel in changing times. As one middle-aged woman sensibly explained her weekly visit to her institutionalized mother:

> When I was a young girl, my mother would take me with her whenever she visited my grandmother in a nursing home. Often she would leave me alone with grandmother for a short while to give us an opportunity to really "visit" together. It seems to me only natural that when a parent is old and alone, he should be seen as often as possible and helped whenever he needs help. I always take my daughter with me when I visit my mother. She is only a teenager, but she can understand that grandma should be seen often. She likes to share what happens in school with my mother, and I often leave them alone while I attend to errands, the same way as my mother used to do. I hope that this means something to my daughter, and perhaps she will teach her children to visit with me when I am old.

4. ECONOMICS OF AGING AND FAMILY RELATIONSHIPS

FINANCIAL CONDITIONS of the elderly have improved markedly within the last four decades compared to what they were earlier in the century. And yet, even today, for many of the elderly the level of their income falls far below their special requirements and leaves much room for improvement.

A review of the early provisions made by government for financial support of the needy aged proves that they were niggardly, failing to meet even essential needs, while eligibility requirements for the granting of assistance did almost nothing to assure respect for the dignity of the recipient. We now see that the elderly, as well as certain other groups in the population, are entitled, as their right, to an income which is sufficient to cover their basic requirements. We are becoming aware that the absence of such an income affects every facet of the older person's life and many of our own—his feelings about himself, his status in society, and his relationship with members of his family, apart from his nutritional and medical needs. It is this better understanding of the consequences of poverty that brings about a more thoughtful consideration of the problems which we know it can create, of the measures available to deal with it, their adequacies as well as their inadequacies, and of the provisions necessary to deal with the problem.

Numbers Affected by Inadequate Income

What are the financial resources available to today's elderly? How far do these resources meet their essential needs? How many of the aged can be said to be in need? To what extent do the existing measures provide an acceptable income?

Studies made by the Administration on Aging of the U.S. Department of Health, Education, and Welfare have established minimum acceptable standards: $3,000 for a couple and $1,500 for a single person living alone or with nonrelatives. The same studies indicate that over one half of the elderly exist on an income which is insufficient to meet these standards. In fact, the income of many of them falls even below what the U.S. Department of Agriculture considers necessary if one is to follow a low-cost food budget, and below the level which is considered essential in order to meet emergencies.

This poor standard of living does not apply to all the elderly. Some of them have a comfortable income, a fact which must be kept in mind in any discussion of the specifics of the economic condition of the aged. However, a substantial number of all elderly (over one third of the total) fall below the poverty line. For them, unrelieved poverty remains a grim reality, adding insult to injury. What does it feel like to spend one's later years trying to manage on so little? For many of the elderly, there is no way in which they can relieve their situation by their own unaided efforts. They are defeated by their years or by the disabilities which often accompany old age. The "final solution" can be very long in coming!

Development of Governmental Assistance— the Social Security Act

Let us look at the present-day provisions for financial assistance by the government and examine the measures taken for their improvement. Because poverty is a social disease, the approach to it through the Social Security Act, promulgated in 1935, marks an important milestone in social legislation in this country. This act accomplishes a number of important purposes: (1) it is based on the principle of universal prepaid insurance, appplied to all persons of a certain age, regardless of their income; (2) in so doing, it eliminates the means test and with it the stigma of a charitable handout or dole; (3) it stresses and highlights the dignity of the individual, stimulating his self-respect as well as his status as a participant by right; (4) it reflects his past contributions, which confers on him the legal right to at least partial support when he can no longer be productive.

It was hoped that with the passage of the Social Security Act, the older person would no longer be a burden on his children, or have to appeal for the charity of a public or voluntary agency—alternatives which have been recognized as detrimental to the older person's well-being physically, mentally, and spiritually. At the same time, he would no longer be compelled to deprive himself of necessities, as in darker times, or live in fear of being unable to meet emergencies. All this, it was hoped, would give him a feeling of independence and replace discouragement with encouragement—life would again have dignity.

Social security is recognized as an important forward step and, as an integral part of our social structure, without the slightest risk of repeal. Despite its benefits, however, the hopes it raised have not been fulfilled for many of the elderly. There are still among them many who are unable to meet their essential needs on the amounts allowed. It it true that social security benefits were not intended to cover total living expenses, but rather to supplement available income. As previously pointed out, however, for many of the elderly they often do represent the main, and sometimes even the total, income. As a result, this group must continue to turn to their children or to a public agency for supplementation.

Recognition of these deficiencies led to periodic legislation to liberalize the payments. Even with the increased benefits, however, income fails to keep pace with rising costs, either in absolute or relative terms, and thus fails to assure the security that the act was intended to provide. In many instances, the amount of the benefits falls below the minimum budgetary requirements set by the U.S. Department of Health, Education, and Welfare. There are still many persons over 65 who are disheartened because they are unable to meet their needs with the limited income and resources at their disposal.

Need for More Productive Steps to Meet the Needs of the Elderly

The inadequacies of current provisions for the aged have been sensed by many community leaders, and by legislators moved by the welfare (or lack of it) of the elderly. Bills have been introduced in the Congress which would remove the statutory limitations on earnings in old age, which so often act as deterrents to the individual's accepting employment, for fear of reducing or losing his social security benefits.

The late Senator Robert F. Kennedy proposed a 50 percent increase in benefits so as to meet more nearly the actual needs of the elderly, but that still awaits legislative sanction. The National Council on the Aging has reminded us that income derived from social security benefits falls below the official definition of poverty and that, according to this definition, "some five to ten million people live in poverty, and that the latest increases granted [in 1967] by the House fix the benefits at still below the poverty level." Feeling that the elderly have "a right to share in the prosperity they helped to create," the Council contends that social security benefits should be considered not only in relation to the cost of living, but to the standards of living.[1] Even the increases granted in 1971 fail to achieve this objective.

A proposal by Wilber J. Cohen, former Secretary of Health, Education, and Welfare, advocated a federally financed system of income payments for the elderly according to need, as means to overcome any rise in the cost of living.[2] The precarious condition in which many of the elderly find themselves with a static minimal income is underlined in the projected estimate that those who retire in 1971 in the middle-income group may well drop to the poverty group in fifteen years.

The importance of the issue of an adequate income for the elderly was impressed on us by the fact that during the 1968 presidential elections, the nominees of both parties endorsed the need for automatic increases in social security benefits to

[1] Sprague, p. 1.   [2] Cohen, p. 17.

keep pace with the cost of living, and for reduction and eventual elimination of the current restrictions on earnings.

New steps undertaken and those under consideration by the
Administration are hopeful signs of forthcoming improvements. In addition to granting the across-the-board increase
in benefits, there is under consideration automatic adjustments
of benefits to correspond to any rise in living costs; increases
in the amount which can be earned by beneficiaries without
reduction of benefits; increase in the benefit base; and more
equitable treatment of the more vulnerable groups among the
aged, such as widows, veterans, persons over 72, those disabled
in childhood, men retiring at the age of 62, and dependent
parents of disabled and retired workers.

Some of these changes have been put into effect, presumably
as a piecemeal measure. Despite this augury for the future,
there persists a significant lag between the actual needs of the
elderly and acceptance of the obligation to meet these needs.
According to the testimony by Bernard E. Nash, executive
director of the National Retired Teachers Association–American Association of Retired Persons, on the Health, Education,
and Welfare appropriations bill,

While the 1971 fiscal year budget request for the Administration
on Aging is $32 million, or $3,640,000 more than the 1970 appropriation, it falls far short of the $54,650,000 authorized by
Congress. . . . This attitude of the Administration has ignored
the intent of Congress, frustrated the desires and needs of older
Americans, and failed to recognize the social and economic impact on the country of increasing numbers of older persons.[3]

It is evident that much more remains to be done to effect an
improvement in the financial situation of the elderly. The

[3] "Nash Cites 'Penny Pinching' by H.E.W. Neglect in Programs,"
p. 1.

elderly are more and more aware that social security benefits even when combined with private pensions—inadequate as these often are—too frequently do not suffice to meet the ever escalating cost of living.

Perhaps the most hopeful sign is that groups of the elderly —the consumer groups—are beginning to voice their disillusionment over the failure of the affluent society to manifest a greater concern for their needs. They are beginning to develop a pride and solidarity as a group and have demonstrated their ability for organized action. At one meeting, for instance, they spoke up about the exercise of what they called "Senior Power" in publicizing their plight. They have organized demonstrations to promote legislation and to protest inadequate action on their behalf. The extent of this "Senior Power" can be judged from the fact that in 1968 those 65 years of age and over cast 65 percent of the votes as compared with 51.1 percent cast by those who were 21 to 24 years old.[4]

Roots of Financial Difficulties

What are some of the factors which are responsible for the deplorable financial condition in which so many citizens find themselves in the terminal years of their lives?

As indicated earlier, some of these difficulties are the result of changes from an agricultural to an industrial society, from advances in technology which make obsolete skills which have been acquired in the course of a lifetime. Perhaps an important contributing cause is the prevailing favoritism for youth and productivity. There is a misleading touch of romance about it! This attitude seems to presuppose that the old and the

[4] "Voting and Registration in Election of 1968," p. 192.

wrinkled must give way in employment for the young and their vigor. The fallacy also presupposes that the government cannot provide for the old because of its preoccupation with the young. Added to the constraints which are imposed by society and affect the welfare of the elderly is the fact that what with limited income and the expense of raising a family, many people have little opportunity to save enough from their earnings to be independent in retirement, while the cost of living becomes progressively higher.

To justify inadequate provisions for the elderly, some argue that old age brings with it a reduction of many of the expenses of earlier years. True as this may be, it fails to recognize that these reductions are more than balanced by other expenses which are increased, such as the cost of medical care due to the greater frequency and longer duration of illness in this group. This is especially true when they live apart from their families.

The conditions enumerated above apply to most people. There are, however, certain groups among the elderly who are particularly vulnerable.

Among the naturalized citizens who are 65 or older today, there is a considerable proportion who brought with them not only foreign languages, mores, beliefs, and traditions which are not easily altered, but also different experiences and skills. These may not be readily adaptable to employment conditions in this country. As a result, workers with skills which may have been adequate in the old country, found that they had to accept employment in the ranks of the unskilled, failing an opportunity to reeducate themselves. Their level of wages during their working lives was thus often lower than that prevailing among the rest of the population. Add to this the fact that when they were at the height of their earning capacity, such economic tragedies as the depression of the thirties exhausted whatever resources they might have accumulated.

EFFECTS OF RETIREMENT

While it is abundantly clear that these conditions have a bearing on the financial difficulties of a significant proportion of the elderly, the most depressing factor influencing the economic status of this group, however, is the practice of mandatory retirement at a fixed age. This practice came into being with the passage of the Social Security Act, which legislated 65 as the age when one should be considered old, with the implication that his productivity is no longer worth the wages paid to him.

The availability of social security benefits, providing a small replacement of normal occupational income, helped to salve the conscience of capricious employers as men were relieved of their jobs, and made it easier to turn away from the hardships and anguish to which employees out in the cold were too often subjected.

Many secondary reasons have been advanced to justify the practice of retiring older workers while they are able to continue working, such as the need of the younger workers for more timely employment opportunities; the need for "new blood" in commerce and industry; and the progressive slowness of the older person to adjust to changing requirements. But these reasons may or may not apply in individual cases although the practice is to generalize inflexibly. At most, they are only rationalizations and excuses. Meantime, the illogical removal of the older worker from the labor force is proceeding apace. Statistics indicate that the number of persons over 65 in the labor force decreased from three fourths of the total in 1900 to one sixth in 1970.

What is often lost sight of is that strict adherence to such practice may be shortsighted on the part of the employer as well as detrimental to the economy in general. The employer is deprived of the knowledge and skill of the experienced worker while spending money on training the younger replacement. At the same time, the retired worker subsists in many instances on an inadequate income. As a result, he not only fails to produce goods, but is compelled to consume less.

The shortsightedness of the policy of compulsory retirement is demonstrated most forcefully, and is particularly destructive, when applied to employed professional workers. Here, neither the requirements of technological changes, nor significant decline in physical stamina, nor the pressure to make room for the younger generation plays a role, since there is a scarcity of qualified personnel in almost all of the professions. The proof of the shortsightedness of this policy lies also in the fact that self-employed professionals continue to work successfully well beyond the age of 65.

The practice of compulsory retirement at a given age persists even where there are serious shortages of trained personnel. There are, of course, isolated instances where the need is particularly acute and where a few individuals past the so-called "retirement age" are retained for short periods. In other instances, such as in social work, agencies resort to nonprofessional replacements to handle the delicate problems of human needs, while adhering strictly to the rule governing retirement. We might also mention the case of military leadership which is often recalled out of retirement to help achieve victory. Herein lies a lesson for us.

As we view the scene, we are reminded of George Bernard Shaw's remark in *Back to Methuselah:* "It is now absolutely certain that the political and social problems raised by our civilization cannot be solved by mere human mushrooms who decay and die when they are just beginning to have a glimmer of the wisdom and knowledge needed for their own government."

PRETIREMENT PLANNING

The reactions of individuals to mandatory retirement differ as they do to any other situation which confronts them. There are those who welcome retirement when it comes, as well as those who choose to retire, if they can, before reaching retirement age. At times, early retirement is chosen for reasons of health. Among those who retire before age 65, the decision to do so is usually arrived at when income from all sources is sufficient to maintain an acceptable standard of living.

The report of a study of factors which influence the degree of satisfaction with retirement status indicates that "nearly seventy percent of all men who retire as planned are content with their lot, as compared with less than thirty percent who retired involuntarily because of ill health or loss of job." [5] Thus, the worker's satisfaction with his retirement status is determined in part by his economic readiness, but also to a considerable degree by the fact that it is voluntary rather than imposed from the outside.

Despite the fact that there is a small percentage of people who find it desirable to retire before age 65, most people place a high value on working. They may be motivated by the need for the income, by their wish to provide for their children in their will, or because they love their work. In

[5] Neugarten, p. 9.

any event, most men expect and prefer to "die in harness," and often react negatively to any interference with their continuing employment. While the eventual prospect of retirement is in their consciousness long before it occurs, they are often able to deny its inevitability until it is actually upon them, and act as if it will never come to pass. The reaction, when the time comes to face it, is often so severe that it has become known as "retirement shock."

We are now recognizing more understandingly the severity of "retirement shock" and are trying to mitigate its effects in advance through discussions with workers. Preretirement planning provides the worker with information as to his rights under the various governmental programs, advice as to financial planning for the future to take better advantage of postretirement income, as well as a discussion of possibilities for part-time or temporary employment.

Workers react favorably to such preretirement discussions in most instances, viewing them as an indication of the employer's interest in their welfare. However, in order to be effective, such planning must begin well in advance of the actual retirement date. When indoctrination and consultation begin early, they improve the worker's response by reducing the anticipated threat of insecurity. According to a report issued by the Drake University Preretirement Planning Center, a follow-up of participants in such an effort indicated that they used the information obtained to good advantage, becoming involved in many ways in planning for the retirement years. A most important finding was the fact that almost three fourths of them "expected post-retirement employment, with one third of those expecting employment to be full time." [6]

The Drake University Preretirement Center also conducted

[6] "Benefits of Planning in Preretirement Years," p. 50.

a study to determine the extent of preretirement planning programs in various fields of endeavor. The study disclosed that
there is "an active interest in preretirement planning, but
there are not many areas in which much has been done." [7]
There are indications, however, that the federal government,
a large employer of labor, is beginning to take a more active
interest in preretirement planning for its employees; indeed,
it has requested the manual of the Drake University Preretirement Center to use as a guide. [8]

Other experiments are being conducted in an effort to
minimize retirement shock. Some employers considerately arrange for gradual reduction in the days or hours of work to
bridge the gap between the accustomed full-time employment
and the retirement to follow. The U.S. Department of Agriculture is experimenting with "trial retirement." This gives
the worker an opportunity to return to work if he is dissatisfied with his retirement status. The idea is new, and no
evaluation of its effectiveness is as yet available.

Some of these measures bring favorable results in individual
instances. The number of employers who have adopted them,
however, is comparatively small. Much more needs to be
done.

Impact of the Economic Background on the Psychosocial Needs of the Elderly

It is important to keep in mind that the problems of poverty
and the stresses and strains of retirement have by-products
which influence more than the older person's reaction to his

[7] "Drake Preretirement Center Conducts National Survey," p. 7.
[8] "Federal Government to Use Drake Preretirement Manual," p. 7.

inadequate income. Economic repercussions on himself and members of his family do not encompass the whole area of difficulties which are inflicted on him or them. There is the additional question as to what extent economic inadequacy and retirement practices affect the individual's mental, emotional, and spiritual health and his ability to achieve a satisfactory social adjustment. No matter how useful preretirement counseling may be in helping to plan the financial arrangements for the future, it fails, in most instances, to help in the emotional reaction of the individual to the feeling of failure and uselessness which retirement brings. This is an area whose importance has as yet received little recognition in existing preretirement planning programs.

LOSS OF STATUS

Through the work in which he was engaged for many years, the individual was able to fulfill what society expected of him, and what he had been taught was the responsibility of an independent, self-reliant person. This is what he wanted for himself and this is what he, in turn, inculcated in his children, deriving pride and satisfaction as he watched them arrive at independence and the ability to conduct their lives in the way that was expected of them.

Because of this ingrained philosophy and tradition, the retired worker, even though his retirement is due to circumstances beyond his control, cannot escape the conviction that his worth has been diminished, and that he can no longer live in the way to which he was accustomed and which he would have wanted to continue. The feeling of inadequacy this creates brings him face to face with the realization that he is indeed becoming old.

Deprived of the prestige which he enjoyed while working,

he may feel that others must also regard him as "not amount-
ing to anything." One often hears the older person say, "Nobody cares when you are old; you are in excess." Unfortunately, the attitude of society tends to increase this feeling of
involuntary worthlessness. This may explain why older people
so often seek employment after retirement, even though it
may be at low pay.

The difficulty which the elderly experience in their inability to find work and to admit their need to depend on
outside assistance is amply demonstrated in the case of Mrs.
Blau:

> Mrs. Blau, an attractive, well-preserved older woman
> with a regal bearing, came to the family agency to ask for
> vocational counseling and a possible job referral. She spoke
> easily, evidently proud of her rich background—college
> education, business experience, and her achievements in
> her chosen career. She had lost her position when the busi-
> ness in which she was employed went out of existence.
> Since that time she had difficulty in securing another job.
> "You know how it is when you reach 60," she said. She
> thought perhaps the agency would use its influence in
> giving her an opportunity to continue working.
>
> The worker agreed that it was hard to secure a job when
> one gets older, but unfortunately the agency could do
> little to help her in the way she desired. Mrs. Blau ap-
> peared not to hear, repeating over and over again how
> frustrating it was not to be able to find a job.
>
> It was only when the worker commented that it must
> be difficult to draw on accumulated savings, since for most
> working people such savings do not last indefinitely, that
> Mrs. Blau was able to admit how really important it was
> for her to begin working again and that, as a matter of
> fact, her savings were exhausted and she was without

funds. Hastily she added that she was beginning to see that her idea of getting a job might be just a "pipe dream" and that she might need help for a short time until she became eligible for social security.

In an attempt to help Mrs. Blau to face reality, the worker questioned whether she had discussed this matter with the public agency, which might be able to help her, but Mrs. Blau felt that she could not do this since it would mean accepting charity. As the worker explained Mrs. Blau's right to such assistance on the basis of having paid taxes, Mrs. Blau agreed to make an application.

Mrs. Blau returned to see the worker a few days later to say that she had made the required application but must bring her birth certificate to the public agency. She apologized for not having told the truth. "I am nearer 70 than 60. I guess there is no use thinking about a job." It was difficult for her to admit that she needed financial assistance, she said, and she was grateful that the worker helped her to face things as they are and not to continue to pretend that they were otherwise both to herself and to others. She was relieved now to know that she could follow the advice of the public agency worker and apply for social security benefits, and that the public agency would be able to supplement if the amount granted were not sufficient.

MEANING OF DEPENDENCE

The reaction to their inescapable need to become financially dependent differs among different individuals, just as the individuals themselves differ. How it will affect any particular person is determined by a variety of factors, among them the extent to which independence and self-reliance influenced his life, his feelings about himself, as well as his relationship to those who surround him.

Independence is universally important and inculcated in the individual from his earliest years. In fact, it is of such importance that it is recognized as one of the three essential requirements in the upbringing of a child in such a way as to insure the preservation of his mental health—the other two being warm love and reasonable discipline.

Preparation in earlier years for adult independence is one of the basic imperatives as man progresses and assumes responsibility not only for himself, but for his family as well—and perhaps for others less fortunate. By example and precept, the parent teaches his offspring the value of independence at the proper time. The effectiveness of his role as a parent is determined, at least in part, by his own independence as a self-reliant man. The possibility and near certainty of the loss of self-reliance in the later years call for an adjustment to a severely changed way of life, of which dependence on the generosity of others is an inescapable part.

Effect of Parents' Economic Plight on Children

Not only the older person, but his adult children as well may be confronted with difficult problems caused by the parent's inability to cope with the challenges of old age and with his dependency needs. Even recognizing that their parent's emotional dependence represents an attempt to adjust to a difficult situation, they may, nevertheless, at times recoil from the heavy burden it imposes on them.

So far as financial dependence is concerned, there is ample evidence that close ties often bind the two generations. Adult children, aware of their parents' financial predicament, often assume their responsibility willingly and extend help when needed. There are, of course, instances when, despite their genuine desire to be of help, they are frustrated by their inability to do so.

It is much more difficult for the adult children to cope with the emotional dependence of their parents. The middle-aged man is particularly vulnerable. Because of the increased longevity, he may at times be confronted with two generations of older relatives—grandparents as well as parents—who may need his financial as well as his emotional support. These pressures occur at a time when he still has to provide for his own family. In addition, he may be acutely aware of prevailing retirement practices and the prospect of his own retirement in the not too distant future. Added to all this is the reaction to witnessing the impact of old age on a person close to him, which brings forcibly to mind what approaching old age foreshadows for him.

The complexity of the problems which confront adult children is illustrated by Mr. Green's story:

When Mr. Green was 53 years old, he found that his parents' savings were exhausted, and that their social security benefits were inadequate to meet their requirements.

Mr. Green's family expenses had been heavy. His wife had been ill at frequent intervals throughout their married life. Heavy medical expenses and the education of their four children left him with minimal savings even though he practiced the strictest economy.

Mr. Green was aware that his own retirement was approaching very swiftly and that he must provide for his later years out of his current earnings. As he put it, he could, of course, count on his children to help, should the need arise, but he did not look forward to this prospect with any pleasure.

He emphasized that he was not complaining about his

own situation. When the time comes for retirement, he will receive a small pension, and the social security benefits will help. With luck, and if no emergencies arise, he might have some of his savings left. He could not help but question, he said, "whether this minimal financial security and possible dependence on children is what one should have at the end of a life of work and savings."

Despite his preoccupation with his own future, he felt he must consider his old parents. His father, who is 80 years old, is deteriorating rapidly as the result of a stroke he suffered not long ago. Knowing that his father dreads the idea of entering a nursing home, Mr. Green contributed to the support of his parents to enable them to remain in their accustomed surroundings. Now, however, he is no longer able to do this, for the kind of attention his father's condition requires, is beyond his means. His father agrees with him that a nursing home is the only solution to the problem.

Mr. Green, aware of his father's feelings about a nursing home, is torn between the needs of his own family and the demands of his father's condition. "I should be able to do more for my father," he says, "but where does my duty lie?"

Those who are charged with the responsibility of helping in similar situations come into daily contact with the anguish which these problems cause for the elderly and for their children. Few parents are unaware of, or insensitive to, the difficulties which their financial dependence creates for their children. In an attempt to justify such dependence, they recall the many sacrifices which they made when they were raising their families. Despite their efforts to understand and appreciate the difficulties their children experience, there remains a tinge of resentment.

On the other hand, adult children do not always consider

responsibility for their aging parents as being in the nature of a reciprocal arrangement. Often they feel that by discharging their duty to their own children—their primary responsibility —they repay whatever debt they owe to the older generation. Even when they thus rationalize their own attitude, they are often left with a nagging feeling of guilt.

EMOTIONAL DEPENDENCE

The reaction to cessation of productivity, to the inability to maintain an independent mode of existence, and to the need to adjust to a painfully changed situation vary with different individuals. Some persist in their effort to retain at least a remnant of their self-reliance in the form of a protective mechanism, conscious as they are of the fact that society frowns upon evidence of dependence in an adult. Others take refuge in the knowledge that their advanced age and the debilitated condition which it often brings, confer legitimacy on manifestations of dependency, and this knowledge makes its acceptance tolerable.

There are also those in whom the need to accept unavoidable dependence creates a conflict between their long struggle to achieve independence and the reality situation which retirement and reduction of income on the one hand and physical infirmities on the other so frequently impose. This conflict often leads to an exaggerated dependence and the demand for increased attention from those who may have had a measure of responsibility for their plight, as well as from others, as if to prove that they can still exercise authority. Such a reaction may occur when the older individual was deprived of the satisfaction of this vital need early in life at a time when such need was normal and understandable, and for which he is now trying to compensate.

The case of Mrs. Chase illustrates such a reaction:

In discussing her childhood, Mrs. Chase emphasizes the fact that she was the "ugly duckling" in her family. She was the only girl in a family of three boys, and good looks were considered by her parents to be particularly important for a girl. Since she could not satisfy this requirement, the parents ignored her—or so she thought— devoting all their attention to the boys.

After her marriage, Mrs. Chase depended entirely on her husband, who humored her and yielded to all her wishes. His death left her incapable of coping with everyday problems and, when confronted with the need to make a decision, she turned to her sons and expected them to decide matters for her. Since her sons lived in different and distant states, any decision that had to be made was made through correspondence with them.

As Mrs. Chase's health deteriorated, she became incapable of attending to her needs, but refused to have anyone come to her home to help her. When the question of entering a home for the aged was broached, she thought it might be the right thing for her to do, but could not make a decision without consulting her sons. They all agreed that it would be the best possible solution, as they felt it inadvisable for their mother to continue living alone under existing circumstances.

The advice, which Mrs. Chase had sought, was now considered by her to be an indication that her sons did not love her and that they wanted to be rid of their problem by "putting her away." She rejected all attempts to make her see that her sons' response was, in reality, the best evidence of their concern for her welfare and safety. Finally, "if that is so," she said, "let one of them come to make all the necessary arrangements and see that I am placed comfortably."

While the case of Mrs. Chase illustrates the heavy dependence of an elderly mother on her children, in other instances the relationship may be aggravated by the parents' utter refusal to accept any help despite the most urgent need for it. Such reluctance is not necessarily the consequence of a strained relationship between the generations. It often occurs in families where close and affectionate ties have been preserved.

The reluctance to seek help may be due to the older person's unwillingness or inability to admit to others, or even to himself, his changed status as evidenced by the need for help. Or it may be due to a parent's intense desire not to become a burden on his children. The elderly parent often says: "I hope that I never have to depend on my children for help or support. I do not want any help from them—they have their own families to consider, and that is their primary responsibility." This feeling is often so strong that even when the parent is confronted with severe hardship, he prefers to apply to a public agency for help, despite the stigma attached to it and his strong reluctance to do so. The desire of the parent not to jeopardize the welfare of his children was amply demonstrated when public assistance regulations demanded strict enforcement of the children's responsibility for the support of their parents. Frequently, the older people preferred to refuse public assistance, despite their need, rather than agree to impose this unpleasant condition on their children.

What the elderly need, for their survival, from their children is evidence of love, interest, and devotion, apart from financial help. In some countries, such as Denmark, for instance, the harmful effect on family unity and the welfare of the elderly produced by the older person's financial dependence on his children was clearly recognized and led to the adoption of governmental help for the elderly long ago, thus enabling both generations to maintain friendly contact without the intrusion of the ugly by-products of financial dependence.

Not all of the elderly react unfavorably to the prospect of becoming financially dependent on their offspring. There are those who take refuge in a dependent role—presumably sanctioned by society for the handicaps of old age—and welcome financial as well as emotional support from their children. Others resolve the problem by self-effacement, meekly seeking nothing and behaving as if they no longer amount to anything and are, therefore, not entitled to anything.

The difficulties here discussed do not apply in all instances. The dependence of the parent does not necessarily create difficulties in the parent-child relationship. Where the relationship is a wholesome one, with love, affection, and mutual respect between the generations, overdependence on the part of the parent, or overprotection by the child, need not and is not likely to arise, as is illustrated in the following situation:

Mr. Law was a well-educated, well-spoken and alert man of over 80. After Mrs. Law's death, the son, feeling that his father could not manage for himself adequately, took him into his home.

As Mr. Law talks about his children, it is clear that he is strongly attached to them; is happy that he was able to give them a good education; and is proud that they have made good use of it and achieved status in the community.

When the first shock following his wife's death wore off somewhat, Mr. Law decided to move out of his son's home despite their affectionate relationship. He discussed his plan of entering a nursing home with his son and daughter-in-law; he emphasized his need to live independently and frankly told them that he feared that his continued stay in their home might eventually create difficulties and seriously jeopardize both their mutually satisfactory relationship and their own family life.

Mr. Law's children reemphasized their desire to have him remain with them indefinitely. However, they respected his right to live according to his wishes. Once his decision to enter a nursing home was made, they cheerfully undertook to supplement his meager income and provide whatever extras were needed to make him comfortable.

The move did not create any strain in their relationship. The children and grandchildren visited Mr. Law frequently, and arrangements were made to have him visit them as often as he desired. Despite the physical distance, Mr. Law remained part of the family.

In this instance, the children's ability to respect Mr. Law's right to make his own decisions and their willingness to help him achieve what he desired were the factors in maintaining a satisfactory relationship whether Mr. Law continued to share the family home or lived in a nursing home.

While recognizing the reasons underlying the need for dependence, as manifested by some of the elderly, and the insistence on maintaining maximal independence, so necessary to others, it is important to keep in mind that the older person's needs and demands may tend to aggravate the strains and stresses between the generations. It is generally accepted in our culture that dependence of the adult child upon his parents, as well as the dependence of the parent on his grown children, is conducive to an unwholesome situation. On the other hand, stress can also be created when an old and feeble parent insists upon maintaining an independent existence, ignoring the danger in which he places himself. It takes a great deal of love, understanding, and tolerance to combat such barriers to coexistence.

5. PATTERNS OF LIVING ACCOMMODATIONS

THE NUMEROUS ADVERSITIES which haunt the later years of life often have serious implications for the older person's ability to maintain his accustomed way of living and may precipitate the need for drastic changes in his living arrangements. The need for such changes may be due to reduced income, deterioration of physical or mental health, or his inability to endure the pangs of loneliness occasioned by the death of the mate. Whatever the precipitating cause, the need for drastic change in living arrangements may cause great concern, requiring a readjustment often fraught with stress and hardship.

Where Do the Elderly Live?

As a background for any discussion of the effect of change in living accommodations on the older person and on his relationship with family members, it is essential to have a clear picture of the living patterns of the elderly in our society. To secure information on this important subject, let us turn to the statistics gathered by the Administration on Aging of the U.S. Department of Health, Education, and Welfare which provides reliable data for 1967.[1]

According to these figures, of the eighteen million people 65 years of age or over, thirteen million lived in family groups with the husband and wife present; an additional million and a half lived independently, and the remainder shared the home of a relative. As can be seen from these figures, his marital status has a significant bearing on the older person's ability to maintain an independent existence in a home of his own and, presumably, to care for his needs. The estimate does not include specific information as to the number of individuals who are able to maintain an independent existence, using instead two categories—those living with a family member, and unrelated individuals. It is reasonable to assume that among these there would be some who are unable to live independently. In both groups, however, the figures confirm what has been shown in the 1967 report, namely, that among those elderly individuals who cannot live alone, the number of those who are over 75 years of age is almost double that in the 64–75 age group.

So far as the number of individuals living alone and remaining able to maintain an independent existence is concerned, their numbers show a decline as we compare those in the

[1] Brotman, "Who Are the Aged: a Demographic View," p. 26, Table 8.

At the time of writing, more recent figures, as revealed in the 1970 census were not yet available. The U.S. Department of Health, Education, and Welfare, however, has made available an estimate of the family status of the older population, dated March, 1970. The distribution given in this estimate differs from the distribution given in the 1967 report, thus making comparisons impossible.

group of elderly who are 75 years of age or older with the 65–74 age group. Advanced age imposes its own requirements. Any living arrangement, satisfactory as it may be at any particular time, cannot be expected to last indefinitely in most instances. Rather, it must be considered in the nature of a temporary arrangement which time and age are likely to change.

This applies not only to the single individual living alone, but also to those who, according to the study, share the home of a relative. Among them, the number of women is three times that of the men. The estimate also points up sharply the larger percentage of women who share the home of a relative. This again confirms the findings in the 1967 report. While statistics fail to disclose the reason for this particular distribution, the figures raise a number of questions. Undoubtedly, part of the answer lies in the fact that women live longer than men, and therefore there are more widows than widowers who might be taken into the home of a relative. Part of the answer may also be that women have more ability to be of help with household chores than men. It is also possible that the arrangement is entered into because women in our society control more of the money than men do and can, therefore, pay for their upkeep in more instances. They may also be expected to remember their relatives in their will. Was this the deciding factor, at least in some of the cases?

Other questions come to mind which have more important significance for the elderly concerned. Was the arrangement entered into because the older person required the particular type of security the relative offered, whether economic, medical, or social? Is the care rendered because of genuine devotion, or because of a feeling of duty? Are the relationships friendly or are they strained, would the older person be better off living somewhere else, and would he as well as the relative be happier with a different arrangement? It is obvious that the answers to these questions cannot be obtained merely by looking at the statistics. We will attempt to arrive at some answers in the discussion which follows.

INSTITUTIONALIZED AGED

Let us consider the 7 percent of the over-65 group who, according to the data issued by the U.S. Department of Health, Education, and Welfare, live in institutions. It can be assumed that most of them are handicapped by physical, mental, or social ailments which made continued independent living in the community impossible.

This small percentage of institutionalized aged has often been cited as an indication that the number of elderly who are unable to maintain themselves in the community is small. In fact, on the basis of figures available for 1967, the number is often referred to as *only* 7 percent, as if to emphasize its insignificance.

The percentage of institutionalized aged, as given in the estimate, is smaller than the percentage given in the 1967 report, namely, about 5 percent. It is reasonable to assume that the difference is due to the fact that this is merely an estimate arrived at after a comparatively short period of time and may not reflect what the number will be on the basis of the actual census. That this may not be an accurate indication is further supported by the known increase in nursing homes, extended care facilities, and homes for the aged since 1967.

Let us consider the implications of this percentage. To begin with, in attempting to emphasize its insignificance we seem to overlook the fact that it represents some 1,310,000 individuals (figured on the basis of the total number of aged in the population in 1967) who have to face the bleakness and hope-lessness of institutional living. Furthermore, if we consider that the aging population numbered over twenty-five million in 1970, then 7 percent would mean that a far larger number of elderly people are in institutions. Moreover, we must also con-sider the fact that members of his family may be affected by the older person's institutionalization. They may not always see institutionalization as a desirable arrangement. There are those for whom it creates a tragic and heart-rending situation which is accepted only because no other alternative is available.

A closer look at the percentage of institutionalized aged reveals that it does not always tell the whole story. Breaking these figures down, we find that the institutionalized aged who are 75 years of age or older represent 14 percent in institutions, as against a little over 4 percent of the institutionalized in the 65–74 age group. Even in the small number of institutionalized aged, as given in the estimate, it is clearly indicated that the number of those who are over 75 years of age is larger than the number of those in the 65–74 year group—550 as against 264. In other words, as the years advance and physical and mental incapacities increase, we can expect that larger numbers of elderly will require institutional care in the future. It is reasonable to predict that among many of the elderly who are able to maintain themselves, will be a number who will be forced to enter an institution as their strength ebbs and neither they themselves, nor their relatives, nor the strangers with whom they reside are able to cope with their needs.

While one may hope that medical science will help to al-leviate some of the distressful ailments of the aged, neverthe-less one has to agree that with the lengthening of the life span, a large number of older people in general, and of those who are 75 or older in particular, will require institutionalization.

Taking all these facts into consideration, it would appear that putting the emphasis on the *small* proportion of elderly in institutions is not only inaccurate, but it indicates a lack of sensitivity to the plight of a group of people who are particularly needful of our understanding and concern. Nor can we disregard the predicament in which the even larger group —those who are related to, and concerned with, the welfare of the elderly person—find themselves.

While we have concentrated our attention on those elderly who often find themselves in need of attention and care from strangers, we must not forget that there are those who are fortunate enough to be able to remain with stable and loving families until the peaceful end of their days. However, the proportion who can look forward to such an ideal old age is unfortunately not large. In some instances, at least, the number could presumably be increased if we could provide housing suitable to their needs, as well as home health services of various kinds. It is the absence of such services that often results in the need for the older person to enter an institution.

As we have pointed out, the large number of elderly people who require institutionalization has resulted in a substantial increase in the homes for the aged and other institutional facilities which have been developing in the community.

Importance of the Place of Residence

The place he calls "home" is as important to the elderly person as it is to all of us. Shelter and food were considered since time immemorial as primary needs. The concept of a home, however, embraces not merely the physical structure, but the place where one lives one's life and the satisfaction which one can derive from it. "Home is where the heart is."

In considering the different living arrangements available for the elderly it is important to appraise them in the light of the individual's needs at a particular time of life and the degree to which they can satisfy his requirements at that time. We thus find that some of the elderly can continue to live in the same house which they had occupied previously, or in a satisfactory substitute. There are others who may be able to maintain themselves in their accustomed quarters, but require a variety of health aids. Finally, there are those elderly who are too frail to remain at home and have no one to care for them; these elderly need some form of congregate living —either a home for the aged or a nursing home.

Thus, the type of living arrangement will be determined to a considerable extent by the individual's needs—medical and social—at any particular time of his life. The degree of satisfaction which the elderly person can derive from his living arrangements, which he either chooses or must accept, will have a bearing on his feelings about himself and on his relationship to others.

PREFERENCE FOR INDEPENDENT LIVING

A review of the literature which concerns itself with the question of suitable housing for the elderly, as well as discussion with individuals who are approaching old age, leaves little doubt that the majority of older people prefer and hope to maintain an independent mode of living in a home of their own. Often, even a discussion of the possibility of living with relatives or in a congregate institution is met with annoyance, vexation, and evidence of profound suffering.

This strong desire for independent living is the established pattern of life in our culture and is part of the general feeling for the need to maintain independence in other areas of life, which were discussed earlier. Some studies indicate that this is the primary factor responsible for the large number of elderly who continue to live independently despite serious handicaps and the difficulties these entail. It has been suggested that this need for independence is the reason that only a small number of elderly in the United States share the home of their relatives as compared with the situation in England, for instance, where it occurs more frequently.

Let us consider what facilities are available for those elderly who can maintain an independent existence and continue to pursue their usual mode of life but who wish to change their living quarters for any one of a variety of reasons. The choice of living arrangement the elderly person will make is often determined by his economic situation and, consequently, his ability to meet the cost involved.

HOUSING FOR THE AFFLUENT ELDERLY

For the affluent elderly there is a variety of living accommodations.

There are those who can continue their accustomed way of life. Others may purchase a home or apartment in the rather expensive retirement communities which have sprung up within recent years. Most of these communities are located in geographic areas where the climate is mild. Those who can afford to meet the cost involved, can maintain a comfortable and carefree way of life. Many of these retirement communities offer transportation, easy access to shopping, household help, and a variety of activities devoted to recreation and amusement. Some have an infirmary on the grounds, and provision is made for medical care as needed. In other instances, the purchase price or monthly payments include medical care for life.

There are other retirement communities which are less

luxurious. Recreational facilities vary from place to place.

The main attraction of these communities for most elderly people is relief from the burdensome chores of maintaining buildings and grounds, a pleasant climate, and the easy companionship of others in the same age group.

The elderly who live in these communities seem to appreciate the comforts. One of the most often mentioned is a feeling of security, since they are able to determine at the time of purchasing or renting their home what their expenses will be; also the maintenance of the outside of the homes and of the grounds is the primary responsibility of the management, thus relieving the residents of a substantial burden.

As one talks to the residents, one becomes aware that even those who like the arrangement react to the need of having had to make the change. They admit that the change, much as they wanted it, was not an easy one. As they put it, "We all have ties elsewhere, and it was not easy to uproot ourselves." Nevertheless, they find that it is possible to make new friends, for "we are all in the same boat." The variety of activities which are made available enables them free choice of those in which they may be interested, and it is in this community of interest that friendships form. "To be happy in such a community," they say, "you need to want to join groups. Loners would not be happy here. There is more to living here than merely appreciation of the nice weather." They also point out that "as one gets older, it is important to accept the fact that one cannot do as much for oneself as one did previously, and agree to let others provide some of the creature comforts, and take life easy."

Frequently, the migration of the older people to the Sun Cities of our Southern communities is initiated by members of their families with emphasis on the benefits of a warm climate and the companionship of others of the same age. Undoubtedly, in many instances, the plan is motivated by a genuine concern of the children for their parents' welfare, and, when necessary, they are willing to finance the move. There are those, however, who by removing the parents a considerable distance from themselves, at the same time remove themselves from the responsibility of a more intimate involvement. By so doing, they can truthfully say that they cannot visit as frequently as they would like.

The parents too can rationalize the children's infrequent visits, citing distance and expense, reasons which have enough truth in them for comfortable self-deception.

Whatever reason the children might have, such an arrangement can in some instances aggravate the problem of the older person's separation from family and friends. There is evidence that some authorities feel that the separation is acceptable to the parents and they prefer living in these pleasant surroundings. One cannot help but question, however, whether if given a choice without being subjected to pressure, well-meaning as such pressure often is, the elderly would in all instances choose the pleasant weather, blue sky, and sunshine in preference to close association with their children.

Because Florida has such a high proportion of elderly who have migrated there following retirement, an attempt was made to secure information about the parent-in-the-South and the child-in-the-North relationship as observed by social agencies there. It was not surprising to find that the relationship varies but little from what is found when parent and child live in closer proximity, and that the whole gamut of feelings and relationships can be detected.

Some of the younger generation exhibit genuine concern for their parents' welfare. They are in constant touch with them and visit as often as they are able. Others, in discussion with the social workers interested in the older person's welfare, readily admit relief at not having to be burdened with the day-by-day care.

The attitudes of the parents are also varied, exhibiting the same traits that characterized their relationship with their children in the past. These attitudes become exaggerated when illness strikes. Some of the elderly become demanding, insisting that their children come to see them, even when the illness is a minor one and the distance the children have to travel is great. Others show an unwillingness to burden their children, insisting that the true state of their health be kept secret, even when their condition is serious. They want to spare their children the worry and the expense of a long trip, they say. Some retain their feeling of independence, wanting to manage their own affairs, while others want to lean on their children and demand help in attending to even the smallest details. Still others are grateful for any evidence of interest and concern the children manifest, but are not overtly demanding.

HOUSING FOR THE NONAFFLUENT ELDERLY

Many retirement communities are out of financial reach for many of the elderly. Those who, for reasons of economic stringency or declining health, can no longer maintain their accustomed living quarters, may move to less expensive accommodations. For the most part, these are situated in congested areas of the big cities and provide only inadequate facilities. These accommodations have become known as "ghettos of the elderly." It is here that we find so many elderly persons, living in the run-down hotels of our big cities which are euphemistically referred to as "senior citizens' hotels."

While this arrangement, undesirable as it is, may present the only possible solution for some of the elderly, one cannot help but be conscious of the dejection and hopelessness of the inhabitants as they sit hour after hour in the shabby lobbies, or on the benches of a near-by park, dispirited and bored. The only ray of comfort which enlivens their lives is a visit from one or another of their children, who drop in on their way to more pressing and important activities.

Not all of the elderly, however, are even that fortunate. Some of them may have no children, relatives or friends. Others may have children, but, as one old lady put it:

I keep a tight grip on my hurt feelings when I do not see any of my children, or hear from them for weeks at a stretch. I try to remember that they are busy with their household, with their families, and with the various recreational activities which are to them an essential part of their lives. So, when I do see them, I never reproach them, but tell them how glad I am that they were able to come. It is not easy, but that's what growing old means; nothing is easy.

As interest in the welfare of the elderly increased, there developed a better understanding of their needs in all areas of living, including their need for special help so far as housing is concerned.

There are many of the elderly who are not sufficiently handicapped to require institutional care, but who find it difficult to manage an independent existence in the home to which they are accustomed unless they have some household help. The amount and kind of such help will vary with the age and physical condition of the individual. To meet the needs of this particular group, we see the development of specialized aids, such as housekeeping services, part-time help for miscellaneous chores and errands, meals-on-wheels, and various other helpful arrangements.

The younger group among the aged, those who are just entering the period of life known as old age, can be considered in most instances as essentially self-maintaining. They may find, however, that the housing designed for the general population is unsuitable. As age advances, more safety devices need to be provided, such as nonslip floors, bathtub grab bars, extra locks for safety, suitably located light outlets and switches, as well as kitchen shelves within easy reach. Many such structural changes must be made when the building is being constructed.

The very old, while they may not require the kind of care given in nursing homes, would nevertheless need to have medical and nursing facilities within easy reach to meet emergencies. They would also need provisions for relief from heavy household chores, as well as some community food preparation.

To meet the needs of this group, special apartments appeared to be the best possible solution. Since 1929, when the first apartment house for the aged, known as Tompkins Square Houses (in New York City), was constructed by the Association for Improving the Condition of the Poor, we have seen the expansion of such facilities. By the middle of 1967, there were in New York City, for instance, some 200,000 units specially designed for, and occupied by, the elderly. Since that time, local authorities with the aid of the federal government have had under construction in New York City an additional 269,000 units of low-income housing, half of which were specifically designed for the elderly.

As the movement for planning special housing grew, it became apparent that several aspects of the older person's needs had to be taken into consideration. There was, for instance, considerable discussion on the perennial question as to whether the elderly are happier living with others of their own age group, or whether they prefer to be part of the total community in close proximity to younger ages.

It soon became apparent that no single answer was possible, for the desires and the needs of the elderly differed. There were those who wished to be close to the young so as to benefit from the enthusiasm and stimulation which youth can provide. This desire persists even though experience has shown that in the majority of instances it is difficult to maintain close interaction between the old and the young. Even when they live in the same apartment house, the old and the young tend to make friends among those of their own age.

To meet the different requirements, therefore, housing for the elderly tends to be of two different kinds. In some instances, a number of apartments specifically designed for the elderly are set aside in a house which caters to a mixed population. In other instances, special apartment buildings are constructed with the needs of the older person in mind.

Since the aim of special housing is the maintenance of self-sufficiency for as long as possible, it was learned that location is of great importance. It should be within easy access to shopping, recreational facilities, and places of worship, with convenient transportation to medical facilities, as well as for visiting friends and relatives.

Within the housing itself, whether it be in special apartments or in an apartment house to be occupied exclusively by older people, there appears to be a need for special equipment. This requirement is determined by the age group to which the elderly belong.

Effects of Relocation

Important as the provision of specially designed living quarters is for the welfare of the elderly, it nevertheless raises some problems inherent in the need to relocate older people. The elderly, as a rule, are opposed to change. What the readjustment may involve in some instances and the older person's reaction to it, even when it is undertaken with the aim of improving living conditions, are illustrated by Mrs. Sims:

Mrs. Sims, a 66-year-old lady, explained that she came to the neighborhood as a bride, and continued living in the same apartment after her husband's death.

For the past few years, however, her bad eyesight and severe arthritis have made it difficult for her to climb the stairs to her apartment. Neighbors were very kind, she said, and often offered to go marketing for her. She is afraid to impose on them too much, so she often gets along without necessities. She never asks the neighbors to do anything for her, but they insist on helping.

When it was suggested to Mrs. Sims that arrangements could be made to move her into a new development, where she could have an apartment on the ground floor, where there was a grocery store nearby, and a park area where she could enjoy sunshine, she was at first quite interested and even enthusiastic about the prospect.

After thinking it over, however, Mrs. Sims decided to reject the offer, saying that she preferred to remain where she was. She was used to the old neighborhood and to the people whom she knew there. She would feel lost in the new place, she said, and it would be best for her to remain where she was as long as she was able to manage.

On the other hand, there are instances when conditions are such that a change of neighborhood, if not looked forward to eagerly, nevertheless can be accepted. For instance, if long-time friends or neighbors no longer reside in the locality, there appears to be little incentive for the older person to remain there. Similarly, when neighborhoods change radically as different ethnic groups move in, which is often the case in big cities, there is little reason for the older person to remain in the same locality among people whose language, customs, and interests are different from his.

As our discussion indicates, there is no single best possible answer to the problem of suitable living quarters for the elderly. While new apartments built specifically for their comfort and safety would appear to be a satisfactory solution for some, for others it would mean that they were being subjected to the stressful effects of relocation and adjustment to unfamiliar surroundings and new people. While there are those who may reject a move to better quarters, as Mrs. Sims did, others are depressed as they witness the destruction of their neighborhood, which they say brings nearer the realization of their own inevitable destruction. Perhaps the only answer should be provision of the kind of living quarters which the elderly can accept when they are ready to abide by their final decision.

Recognizing the importance which independent living has for the elderly led to the development of several programs to meet the needs of those older people who do not require institutional care but who are unable to maintain themselves without some form of supervision. In one instance, a home for the aged (the Jewish Home and Hospital for the Aged in New York) established a special apartment house for the elderly, under continued supervision by the agency, and provision was made for their removal to the institution when they were no longer able to maintain themselves in the apartment.

Another program which aims to provide suitable living quarters with some supervision is that of foster home care. Under this program, elderly people who are able to care for their personal needs, but who must have their meals prepared for them and require some minimal amount of supervision, are placed with private families under the watchful eye of a social agency.

Available Alternatives

Our previous discussion has indicated that some provisions to meet the changing requirements of the older population have been made. Unfortunately, they fail both in numbers and in facilities. What other alternatives are there for those who because of economic necessity, poor health, or the inability to withstand the pangs of loneliness cannot maintain independent living?

SHARING THE HOME OF THE CHILDREN

As one considers where the older person might live when he is no longer able to remain alone, the question which immediately comes to mind is, "What about his children?" Despite the fact that this is apparently a most natural question, such a possibility is not always open to the old person and may even be fraught with major problems for all concerned. Such a plan requires careful consideration of all the factors involved.

As is true in all other situations where the two generations are involved, the nature of their relationship when the parent is old will be determined to a considerable degree by the feelings carried over from earlier years—the unresolved frustrations and stresses experienced by the children in the past, or the persisting authoritarian attitudes of the parent. In addition, the older person's reaction to sharing the children's home is colored by the implied need to give up his independence. One study found that the morale of the elderly was lowest among those who were living with a child.[2]

The elderly person's reaction is due not only to the need to become dependent, but also to his awareness that his own needs differ from those of his children and his fear that this difference might precipitate conflict and tension. Added to this may be the cultural distance between the immigrant father and the native-born son, which operates in some cases, or the distance between the rural parent and his urban child which operates in other situations. To this we might add the explosion of technological knowledge which is rapidly becoming an accepted part of life among the young, but which is alien and often incomprehensible to the elderly.

While we must admit that these differences are real and often stand in the way of a satisfactory adjustment to sharing the living quarters, there is sufficient evidence to prove that such an arrangement is acceptable and works well in some instances. This is particularly true where the relationship between the generations remained close throughout the years of separate living, and where the presence of the parent would in no way interfere with the life of the younger generation.

Among the factors which make the sharing of living quarters difficult and sometimes even impossible, we might men-

[2] Fowler and McCalla, p. 5.

tion crowded conditions in the home, the children's strained financial circumstances, friction with in-laws, the feeling on the part of the older person of not wanting to be a burden or a source of tension. Sometimes, even when the older person makes his home with a married child, changes in the family situation may create the need for a different arrangement. Such was the situation with Mrs. Young:

Mrs. Young shared the home of her unmarried son for a number of years following the death of Mr. Young. She kept house, and the relationship between the two was compatible and friendly. The son was no longer young, and it appeared that the arrangement, so satisfactory to both of them, would continue indefinitely.

When the son suddenly announced to his mother that he expected to get married, Mrs. Young was at first surprised, then became quite disturbed at the prospect of having her living pattern disrupted, dreading the need to move out and find other quarters.

Fortunately, the arrival of her daughter-in-law did not change the situation, as the latter expected to continue working, would be away all day, and would be more than happy, she said, if Mrs. Young would continue living with them and be in charge of the household, as was her wont.

All went well and nothing was said of any impending change. Even when the younger Mrs. Young became pregnant and gave up her employment, she offered to help her mother-in-law, but left all decisions to her. Mrs. Young was happy with the arrangement and looked forward to the arrival of the grandchild.

Shortly after the baby was born, it became apparent that Mrs. Young's room was needed for the baby. It was suggested to Mrs. Young that she would be comfortable on the living room couch, and both her son and daughter-in-law strongly urged her to remain with them.

Mrs. Young, however, was hurt and resentful. She felt that even if she were willing to put up with the inconvenience, the proposed arrangement would eventually lead to disagreements. Rather than risk it, she preferred to move out, find a room with a private family, where she "could have her own room, her own bed, and privacy."

As her plans were discussed with Mrs. Young, she pointed out that she did not know what she could have done if she had not had her social security benefits to supplement her inadequate income. Without them, she said, she would have had no choice but to accept whatever was offered to her.

The social security benefits gave Mrs. Young, as they frequently give to others, a choice as to how her life was to be lived. Choice thus means a feeling of independence which contributes to the individual's feeling of dignity.

This emphasis on the need for independence exhibited by Mrs. Young is not an isolated phenomenon. It is the prevailing pattern of life in our country. And it is well expressed in the attitude of parents who, in discussing the possibility of sharing their children's home, often say that "parents have to know their place in the home of their children to make living together possible."

In Mrs. Young's situation, the change was precipitated not only by the hurt she felt in being asked to give up her room, but also because of the actual lack of space in the apartment. However, while lack of space is an important barrier to sharing the home, it is not the whole answer. Many of the elderly who have had the experience of living with their children felt that they were segregated from the family. Some mention that contact with the children's friends was not encouraged. Others felt that sharing the home imposed on them an obligation which they were in no position to meet.

The women tried to repay their children by attending to such chores as were assigned to them. The men felt that they seldom had an opportunity to reciprocate, except by occasional baby sitting.

There appears to be ample evidence to indicate that, in most instances, neither the old nor the young welcome the prospect of living together. What the older family members want is to maintain their own living quarters and to have frequent and cordial contact with their children. Such contacts, they say, help to assuage their loneliness and provide assurance that help will be forthcoming when needed.

It has been said that "the great majority of old people are in regular contact with their children, relatives, or friends. . . . Where distance permits, the generations continue to shoulder their traditional obligations of elders toward their children, and children toward the aged." [3] Perhaps the most significant part of this statement is the emphasis on "where distance permits." One might question how often distance does permit such close contact in view of the mobility of our population, and how often distance is invoked as an excuse for failure to maintain contact. All those who have had close and intimate contact with elderly people can attest to the frequent absence of such close contact and to the fact that many of them suffer from loneliness.

Congregate Living

Experience points to the fact that when the elderly person is no longer able to care for himself in his own home and does not wish to or cannot share the home of his children, the only recourse open to him is to accept some form of congre-

[3] Blenkner, p. 49.

gate living, often referred to as "institutional care." The term "institutional care" usually refers to two types of institutions: health-related facilities, such as the chronic disease hospital and nursing home, which has previously been discussed; and the home for the aged.

The home for the aged is one of the oldest institutions for the care of the elderly. It is designed primarily for the care of the frail elderly who do not require medical care but need a place to live and the security that someone will be there in case help is needed. The fact that practically every home for the aged is equipped with an infirmary for the care of minor ailments is reassuring to the older person.

As was previously indicated, admission to an extended care facility is arranged at the recommendation of the hospital as part of the total treatment of the patient's ailment, and the older person has, presumably, little to say in the matter. By contrast, the decision to enter a home for the aged is arrived at by the individual himself. Thus, in a sense, the older person exercises a certain amount of free choice in this matter. However, the choice is a "free choice" in only a relative sense in many instances, for the home for the aged is frequently chosen by the older person not because he wants it but because there is no acceptable alternative. In some instances, the choice is made even though the individual is given the opportunity to share the home of his children. He may prefer the dependence on strangers, whose role he sees as being there to help him and provide for his needs, rather than accept dependence on his children.

EFFECT ON THE OLDER PERSON

Whatever the reason for the individual's choice of an institution as a place to spend his remaining years, entering the institution is, in most instances, a traumatic experience and the cause of fears and misgivings. After admission, he may find that the reality is not so bad as he feared—or it may be worse than he expected. At the very beginning, however, he comes face to face with the conviction that he has taken a final and irrevocable step. This is especially true when the home requires the person to surrender all his assets under the terms of a life contract. The realization of the destructive effect of this practice has led many homes to adopt a monthly payment plan, thus giving the individual the freedom to terminate it if he desires to do so.

Even under these circumstances, there are certain elements inherent in the situation which produce an unfavorable reaction and demand an adjustment which is not always easy to achieve. Primary among these factors is that although they have, presumably, chosen to enter the home, in reality the elderly often feel that the decision was forced on them, either directly or indirectly. Thus it is not surprising that they vent their dissatisfaction on the institution, find fault with it, and fail to achieve a satisfactory adjustment. Many of the elderly feel that by entering the home they have lost their dignity and self-respect. As one old man put it, "To see the inscription 'Cast us not off in our old age' on the building or the stationery is ironic. Our very presence here is an indication that we have been cast off by our families, by society, by life itself."

Some of the requirements imposed on the elderly when they enter the home, unfortunately unavoidable though they may be, are difficult for them to meet. To begin with, it means a radical change from the older person's previous way of life and the elderly do not adjust easily to change. There is need to observe rules and regulations which do not always coincide with individual preferences. It means a close association with strangers with whom they have to share intimate details of their lives, even sharing a room in some instances. The fact that, usually, it may be difficult for the home to separate the old person who is frail from the one who is deteriorating, physically or mentally, often aggravates the situation. It compels the witnessing of suffering and abnormalities, which brings the old person face to face with the specter of what might be awaiting him in the future.

The home often fails to provide meaningful free-time activities. While one sees lounges with television sets, these seldom fail to dispel the feeling of hopelessness and gloom. One often finds the elderly merely sitting in front of them, hardly following what is going on. Even when they watch the programs, they cannot help but contrast them with what their previously active life had been.

The most important factor, however, which contributes to dissatisfaction and resentment is the climate of the institution itself and the relationship which is established between the staff and the residents. Too often the attitude of the staff is either disinterested or, at best, condescending. Any infraction of rules is often met not with an effort to handle it as one would with adults, but with scolding as if the residents were recalcitrant children. For instance, there is a tendency in some homes to refer to the residents by their given name. Even when this practice is meant to convey friendliness, some residents consider it to be a lack of respect, especially because of their advanced years, and because the practice is not reciprocal. As one old man put it: "I have been used to being addressed by strangers as Mr. When I first came here and heard a member of the staff call out my first name, I did not think it was meant for me and I did not respond. I suppose I'll have to get used to it, but I do not like it."

Another aspect of the attitude of the staff is often evident in the way they give the residents the necessary physical care. Even when this care is adequate, there is little communication between the staff and the residents, and therefore the old people are denied an opportunity for a real involvement in human contact.

Just how far a dull environment or unsatisfactory relationships with others contribute to the acceleration of the aging process is difficult to determine without more thorough study, since unfavorable effects are often delayed and obscured by a number of other changes in the older person's condition. That the transfer to a more stimulating environment can produce significant improvement, however, is demonstrated in the case of Mrs. Mound:

> Mrs. Mound, an intelligent, well-educated, and gifted person found herself without close relatives at the age of 84. Unable to care for herself, she discussed the situation with a niece by marriage, who visited her from time to time. Not only was Mrs. Mound unable to care for her needs, but she suffered periods of depression so severe that they frightened her. Perhaps, she said, she would be better off in a home rather than in the little room which she occupied and where she had practically no human contact. At least, in a home she would have some companionship, she said.
>
> The niece arranged to have her admitted to a home for the aged, and continued to visit her there. After a while she was able to report considerable improvement in Mrs. Mound's condition. Her aunt, she said, was again her former self—interested, active, taking part in all of the home's activities and demonstrating the leadership qualities she possessed. It was indeed fortunate, she said, that the home had the necessary facilities for all sorts of activi-

ties and a staff interested in promoting their fruitful utilization. Mrs. Mound's age did not prejudice them.

This case illustrates clearly that a satisfactory adjustment is facilitated when the older person enters the institution of his own free will and with the feeling that the environment will be not only acceptable but beneficial. Equally important is the attitude of the administration and the staff which encourages treatment of residents with consideration, respects them as individuals, and takes pains to safeguard their privacy.

Where this atmosphere exists, we find that many of the residents, in discussing their feelings about the institution, express their appreciation of the sense of security which they enjoy, knowing that there is someone to whom they can turn in case of need on a twenty-four-hour-a-day basis, and that attention will be forthcoming. They recognize that restrictions are essential and that these restrictions actually enhance their feeling of security; they interpret them as a sign that there is someone who cares for them and wants to protect them. They appreciate the availability of activities and the freedom which they have in deciding whether or not they wish to participate in them. In addition, they find satisfaction in being in a well-kept, well-run institution.

The different reactions to an institution for the aged as manifested by the residents—contentment, acceptance of the inevitable, or dissatisfaction—are not always provoked by the institution itself, but rather may reflect the person's feelings of satisfaction or dissatisfaction with his lot and with the condition which is responsible for it. It is for this reason that even satisfaction with his new way of life may be disturbed by temporary annoyances; at other times expressed dissatisfactions are often tempered by acceptance and even pleasure derived from associations in the institution and with its activities.

There are times when family members are unable to provide the care the elderly person needs. Concerned with his welfare, and realizing the lack of other alternatives, they are forced to agree to institutional care as the best possible solution to the problem. So far as the older person is concerned, while realizing the reasonableness of the decision, he cannot help but feel that his family rejected him and failed him at a time of need. He may resent the fact that when he suggested entering a home for the aged, they did nothing to dissuade him.

The difficulty he is experiencing in acknowledging that they are in reality not neglecting his needs is demonstrated in the way in which he tries to deny the implied rejection to everyone outside the family circle, and at times even to himself. He constantly emphasizes the closeness of family ties, the attention he receives from the members of his family, and their evident concern for his welfare and happiness.

This positive picture, which the elderly try to project, has been frequently questioned. It has been stated by some that the home for the aged came into existence in response to pressures on the part of the younger generation who were unwilling to care for the elderly. Dr. H. Droller, of the Geriatric Unit of St. James Hospital in Leeds, England, maintains that to him as an individual doctor, "institutionalization is an admission of having failed to keep or bring an elderly patient into the circle of his family." [4] Others too, like Dr. E. M. Bluestone, for instance, feel that the younger generation

[4] Droller, "Institutionalization," p. 104.

often finds it too easy to divest themselves of the burden of care through institutionalization.

While this may be true in some or even many instances, it is not implied that institutionalization is at all times a matter of callous indifference on the part of the young. Often, they resort to it only after prolonged hesitation and when nothing else is available to meet the situation.

There are circumstances when continued care of the elderly person in the home puts an unsupportable strain on the younger family. Such is the case, for instance, when the elderly parent becomes disabled and the children's own advancing age makes his care difficult. Also, strained financial circumstances or crowded quarters often put obstacles in the way of their providing the necessary care, even though they may wish to do so. Again, the illness of a family member may precipitate the necessity for a change, as was the case in Mrs. Child's family:

Mrs. Child is a well-preserved, immaculately groomed 75-year-old lady who uses a cane when walking. Her appearance belies her age.

Mrs. Child occupies a small room in a pleasant small home for the aged, a room which is made even smaller by the massive furniture which Mrs. Child brought from her home. She explained that having her own things made her feel more at home. She spends a great deal of her time in her room, listening to the radio and knitting articles of attire for her grandchildren. She showed pictures of her daughter and grandchildren with evident pride.

Mrs. Child lived with her daughter after her husband's death, and would have continued living there were it not for the fact that her daughter developed an illness which required frequent hospitalizations. Even when her daughter was home, she was unable to give her mother the necessary care. "My daughter never hinted that caring for me was a burden, but I could see how impossible it was to continue this way." It was Mrs. Child who broached the need for her to enter a home for the aged, and after some discussion, both agreed that it was unavoidable.

Mrs. Child gave no evidence of resentment. She did not complain about her present way of life although she indicated that, comfortable as she was, "it is not like having your own home."

The relationship with the daughter continues to be friendly, and other members of the family—grandchildren, cousins, and aunts—visit Mrs. Child from time to time. Relatives and friends take Mrs. Child out for rides, or for an occasional meal, as well as to see the daughter when the latter is too ill to visit her mother. They do all they can to make Mrs. Child's life as pleasant as possible. It is these close contacts, Mrs. Child says, which make living worthwhile.

While Mrs. Child has accepted life in a home for the aged with a minimum of difficulty, and has maintained a satisfactory relationship with members of her family and friends throughout her residence in the home, this is not always the case. There are those who never fully accept the unavoidable circumstances which led to the need of entering a home for the aged. Nor do they indicate that they were able to maintain a friendly relationship with family members following the separation. There was Mr. Adam, for instance:

Mr. Adam showed some reluctance in discussing his relationship with his son and his son's family. His terse comment, "What can you expect from a daughter-in-law?" indicated all too clearly his resentment. "It is best for me to be in this home. When I come to see my grandchildren, I am treated as a guest. If it were not for them, I would never go." In response to a question, he said: "My son is too busy to come to see me, at least that's what he says. If you ask me, he does what his wife tells him to do. He does not care enough to explain to her what he should be doing."

EFFECT ON FAMILY MEMBERS

Institutionalization and its effect on family relationships cannot be evaluated adequately without considering the impact on members of the family as well as on the elderly person. The attitude of the latter is frequently influenced by his own feelings about the matter, which often blind him to the reality of the situation.

Many factors influence the decision of family members to institutionalize their elderly relative. Some of the precipitating circumstances leading to this step have been indicated. There is ample evidence to substantiate the conclusion that the decision to have a parent admitted to a home for the aged is often arrived at only after other ways of solving the problem of his care have been tried and found wanting.

For instance, children concerned with the financial difficulties which the parent might experience in maintaining separate living quarters, or aware that his physical condition might make living alone not only inadvisable, but in some instances even dangerous, may be prompted to offer to share their home. They may find that resulting overcrowding may strain the previously satisfactory relationship, despite the good will of all concerned. Faced with such difficulties, the children may reluctantly come to the conclusion that admission to a home for the aged would be the most advisable course to take, but not wishing to hurt their parent's feelings, they hesitate to suggest it. The older person, vulnerable as he is, may be conscious of the children's attitude, even when this is not put into words, and often must himself initiate the discussion.

The following case illustrates a situation where the care of the older person becomes an intolerable burden:

> Mrs. Frank had been taking care of her mother since the latter was widowed. She had undertaken to do it gladly, feeling that it was the least she could do for her mother, who had always been good to her.
>
> The arrangement worked out well for a number of years. The mother became an integral part of the family, helping with the household chores and the care of the children. As years passed, the mother became incapacitated and was unable to climb the stairs to her room. Her bed was moved into the family living room and, despite the inconvenience this entailed and the restrictions it imposed on all members of the family, they accepted the situation.
>
> It was not until Mrs. Frank herself became ill and required a great deal of attention that the mother broached the subject of a home for the aged as the only solution to their problem.
>
> Despite the fact that Mrs. Frank saw the impossibility of continuing to care for her mother, she was unable to rid herself of a feeling of guilt. "This is the last thing I would want to do," she said, "it is almost as if I sent my mother to the home to die."

There are times when, in a desire to save the parent from the need to enter an institution and, unaware of existing resources which may make such a decision unnecessary, the children go to extreme lengths to keep the old parent with them to the detriment of all concerned. A time comes, however, when they can see no other way of meeting an impossible situation.

> There was Mrs. Blank, for instance. Her middle-aged daughter made an application to an agency for help in

finding a suitable home for the aged for her mother. She disliked doing it, she said, but it was impossible to continue caring for her at home. Her mother was forgetful, left the gas turned on, and she had to depend on neighbors to look in on her from time to time while she herself was away working. She was afraid of an accident, such as a fire, in which case her mother would be helpless. Besides, she felt that one cannot impose on neighbors indefinitely.

It was recognized that some change needed to be made, but the daughter was apparently not yet ready to accept a home for the aged realistically. The discussion was therefore slanted as to what the step would mean to Mrs. Blank and to her daughter.

After some discussion, the daughter was able to admit that she doubted whether she would be able to accept an institution for her mother. "We talk about it, mother agrees that it is the only way out, and as we discuss it, we both cry. The truth is, I need my mother as much as she needs me."

Once this understanding was reached, it was possible to discuss alternatives. It was finally agreed that placing a housekeeper in the home would meet the need and be an acceptable solution for both of them. The daughter did not know that such an arrangement was possible and thought a home for the aged was the only available recourse.

This case history shows a problem similar in many respects to that illustrated by Mrs. Child. However, it indicates a different reaction and a different solution to the problem. Even when such strong ties bind both generations, as shown in these two cases, and children attempt to accommodate themselves to the demands of the situation by making provision for the care of the elderly in their home, a time may come when advancing age and infirmities make it impossible to continue in such close proximity. There are instances when, confronted with such a situation, the older person can accept institutionalization without resentment and the younger generation without guilt. This was the case with Mrs. Child, discussed previously, and in many other families.

In addition to changes necessitated by increased disability as part of aging, there are other factors which make sharing living quarters inadvisable, even impossible. For instance, when the care of the elderly person interferes with occupational pursuits of the grown children or with the essential needs of other members of the family, it is questionable whether such an arrangement is desirable. The older person cannot help but be conscious of the disturbance which his presence causes. Both he and his children may be happier with a different arrangement, if such an arrangement is arrived at by mutual consent.

This does not necessarily mean institutionalization. Experience has demonstrated that sometimes all that is necessary to relieve tension is the presence of a housekeeper on a full or part-time basis (as was illustrated in the case of Mrs. Blank). In other instances, arrangements can be made for a vacation for the person providing the care, or a temporary placement of the older person in a home to give family members a chance to rest. Frequently, family members, having been relieved of the responsibility for a time, are able to resume their care of the parent.

We cannot disregard the fact that financial considerations often are a decisive factor in determining whether or not the parent can be accommodated in his children's home. Even the most genuine concern for the parent's welfare, and the unquestioned readiness of the children to have him share their home, cannot negate the fact that financially they may be unable to do so.

The children are often caught between their desire to help the parent and the realization that their meager resources or inadequate living space make it impossible for them to do so. Into it goes all the conflict between their feeling of obligation to their parent and the needs of their own growing family, which was discussed earlier. When faced with this conflict, a satisfactory decision becomes even more difficult because of society's traditional expectation (an expectation which is slowly changing) that parents are entitled to be cared for in the home of their children. It is not surprising, therefore, that a negative decision gives rise not only to conflict, but to a feeling of guilt.

It is when the decision is determined by the economically strained situation in the children's home that social security benefits have significant value. Social security gives the parent a choice as to how he wants to live—whether to use this income to help pay for an independent household, or to contribute the sum to the children's income and thus relieve their financial situation. Experience has demonstrated that the availability of this income to pay part of their living expenses has resulted in a greater number of elderly people who choose to live with their children, thus avoiding the strain and unhappiness of making a decision which is so often contrary to the wishes of both generations.

There are instances when the care of the elderly parent need not constitute a burden for one child but can be shared among several children. In some cases, the parent gives up his home and spends his time on a rotating basis with each one of his children. Even when this arrangement is entered into because the children want to help and are happy to have their parent with them, it often gives rise to a disturbing situation for the parent, who feels uprooted and unsettled.

In other instances, the children may decide to contribute

to the parents' upkeep. Though satisfactory at first glance, this arrangement often creates difficulties when the economic condition of one of the children changes, and he is unable to continue his contribution and the others may or may not be able to pick up the slack. Furthermore, such an agreement is often responsible for the acting-out of deep-seated sibling rivalries, which may affect adversely their participation in the plan, whether it be to punish a sibling or win the approval of the parent.

The Borden case gives an illustration of the effect of these important, and often unconscious, attitudes:

Mr. and Mrs. Borden were an elderly couple whose three children undertook to supplement their parents' income, thus helping them to maintain the home where they had spent many years of their lives and which meant a great deal to them.

At first, there seemed to be little difficulty in arriving at an equitable arrangement, and the allocation of each one's share of responsibility was made on the basis of their income. It soon became clear, however, that this arrangement could not be adhered to without some modification.

The daughter, who felt that the parents always favored their oldest son, attempted to win some evidence of appreciation by contributing more from time to time than she could actually afford. At the same time, the favorite son found numerous excuses for not living up to his commitment.

The parents made numerous excuses for the son's failure to contribute his share, while at the same time showing little appreciation for what the daughter was doing, even suggesting that she relieve her brother from the too heavy burden he was carrying.

Our discussion of the various types of living arrangements available for the elderly, as well as the discussion of every other aspect of the older person's needs, and the solutions available to meet them, all bring us to the same conclusion, namely, that the elderly, like the rest of us, are individuals with individual needs and desires, and that no one plan, no matter how good it may be, is suitable for all of them. The only way to provide satisfying living for the elderly is to consider each individual situation, evaluate what the person wants for himself, and try to find a solution suitable to meet these individual needs.

6. *ILL-HEALTH AND FAMILY RELATIONSHIPS*

ILL-HEALTH has long been recognized as one of the more pressing problems afflicting the elderly. The miracles of medical science have so far conferred their benefits on the young, eliminating the infectious diseases of childhood, preventing and curing many of the illnesses of the adult population, and making it possible for more people to survive to old age—but failing to affect to any considerable degree the progressive, lingering illnesses which so often plague the elderly.

The persevering nature of these illnesses, coupled with the older person's diminished recuperative powers, results in the need for more attention from the medical practitioners, longer hospital stays, and heavier expenditures on drugs and medical care generally than is the case among younger individuals.

Studies by the U.S. Department of Health, Education, and Welfare show that elderly people average forty-six days of restricted activity and some nineteen days of confinement in bed in the course of a year. For those who are 75 years of age or over—comprising about one third of the total older group—there is an increase in bed disability and restricted activity. The number of visits by physicians per year is also higher when compared with those in the 65–74-year-old group.[1] In other words, the older the patient, the more severe and long-lasting are his illnesses and incapacities. It is therefore not surprising to find that, according to the Social Security Administration, the "average medical bill for an over-65 American was $590 in 1968, a rise of twenty-one percent in a year. For persons under sixty-five, the per capita cost was $195, an increase of only ten percent." [2]

This incidence of illness, duration of disability, frequent deterioration of the physical and mental condition of the elderly, and the rise in medical costs have been drawing greater attention to their medical needs. It is now being recognized that ill-health among the elderly is a major problem with which society has to deal, and one which so far has eluded solution.

Emergence of Interest

Interest in, and concern for, the health of the elderly on the part of the medical profession has been minimal, reflecting the attitude of society as a whole. The approach to this problem was influenced to a considerable degree by the assumption that the illnesses afflicting the aged were to be expected at this period of life, and therefore little or nothing could be done to help them. All too often, the physician's response to the complaints of the sick elderly was: "You are getting on, you know. What can you expect? The machinery is wearing out." This attitude is all too frequent even today.

[1] Brotman, "Who Are the Aged: a Demographic View," p. 20.
[2] "65 + Medical Costs $590, 21% Rise; Non-Elderly Bill $195, up 10%," p. 12.

This equation of old age with illness was so commonplace that the very designation "old age" became a diagnosis in itself. Since "old age" could not be altered, the diagnosis carried with it a hopeless prognosis and constituted a barrier to any attempt at treatment. It also meant that there was little need for the physician to concern himself with whatever further changes occurred in the older person's physical condition, or with his complaints about new discomforts or pain—it all came under the heading of "old age" and meant that nothing could be done to change the situation. As a result, elderly patients frequently developed intercurrent illnesses, which often remained unrecognized, untreated, and were sometimes fatal.

The attitude of the medical profession communicated itself to all those who were involved with the care of the elderly sick. It served to perpetuate the grim, hopeless, and depressing atmosphere which so often prevails in the geriatric wards of general hospitals, as well as in the chronic disease institutions.

Changes in Attitudes

It would be unrealistic to assume that these attitudes were confined to the unenlightened past. They persist in some quarters even today, though fortunately they appear less and less often. Although progress is slow, there can be perceived a glimmer of hope that attitudes are changing. This can be seen in the more frequent use of the designations "long-term illness" and "prolonged illness" which are slowly replacing the old phrase "chronic illness" with its implication of hopelessness.

This emerging trend is due to the concerted efforts of a small group of enlightened individuals who have been vocal in their attempts to spread the concept of "old age" as being a part of our total life span and of the elderly as being entitled to the same consideration and to the same efforts to minimize the ravages of illness as are members of other age groups. In part, it may also be due to the large number of older people among us, so that the very pressure of numbers made it impossible to overlook them or push them aside. As many more families were faced with the problems of elderly relatives, they could no longer regard them as merely members of the anonymous group called "the aged," but saw them as suffering relatives. Consequently, family members became more vociferous in demanding medical treatment for their sick elderly.

The hope that adequate treatment for the elderly will become a reality and accepted as a universal obligation by the medical profession, rests upon a change in the attitude of the teachers of medical students—the future medical practitioners.

Chauncey D. Leake's editorial writer for *Geriatrics*, report on a study at the Langley Porter Neuropsychiatric Clinic of the University of California brings the need for such change into sharp focus. This study found that medical students consider older people "more emotionally disturbed than young people, being dull, apathetic, socially unpleasant, withdrawn, disagreeable, dissatisfied and disruptive of social and family welfare." This description of the elderly is characteristic of the general attitude of the young in our society—part of the "generation gap." Apparently, no thought was given by these young medical students to what lies behind these unacceptable attitudes sometimes manifested by the elderly.

Given this point of view, it is not surprising to find that in indicating their treatment preferences, the care of the elderly was put at the bottom of the list. The article concludes that "this indicates that the aged are the most medically underprivileged minority in our country" and suggests changes in teaching emphasis by stating that "it would be wise to begin early in medical training to inculcate some regard and respect for the medical needs of the ever increasing number of older people which the members of the health professions will be called upon to handle." It would appear that the very words "old age" may be responsible for the negative reactions, since in the same study the same group of medical students indicated their interest in those diseases, such as heart disease, which appeared on the top of the preference list, with apparently little realization that these illnesses are the ones which occur frequently among the old.[3]

Unfortunately, too many physicians, influenced by and sharing the negative attitude of society, consider that work with the elderly is less interesting and less rewarding than work with younger patients. Until this attitude is changed, the young men entering the medical profession and taking their cue from the older physicians will too often choose other areas of medicine as their specialties.

There is ample evidence to indicate that the elderly are acutely aware of this attitude of the medical profession. As a result, they lack a feeling of security in bringing their medical problems to the attention of the physician. Many of them fear that they may not have the money to pay the doctor (this worry has been somewhat eliminated with the passage of Medicare and Medicaid), or that the doctor will not be available when needed. Most important, perhaps, is their feeling that the doctor does not "want to be bothered with them."

Since the root of the problem is the patient's illness, it is to the physician and the professional personnel associated with him that the family must look for the understanding and help they require to deal with a difficult situation.

[3] Leake, pp. 58–59.

They need help in understanding the nature of the patient's illness and its effect on him. They must be helped to see that the demanding attitude so often exhibited by the sick person, his complaints and difficult behavior are symptoms of his suffering, unhappiness, and helplessness, and that they in no way reflect what they are doing for him; neither do they constitute a reproach for their failure to meet all his needs. They must be helped to see that such unreasonable behavior often represents a cry for help and support by a person who can no longer summon his resources—economic, social, and emotional—to handle the difficult problem which confronts him. In addition, family members must be reassured that they are doing the best they can, and that there are realistic limits to what they can do.

Despite the frequent manifestations of disinterest by the medical profession, one can draw some comfort from indications that there is developing a heightened interest in the health problems of the elderly and a recognition that elderly people often respond to proper treatment. We are seeing an increase in medical publications devoted to geriatric medicine in all its aspects. Some physicians are beginning to advocate a more positive—even optimistic—outlook in their dealings with the elderly, and they point to the fact that geriatric medicine is not devoid of either interest or reward, even though it may require a greater investment of time, concern, patience, and skill.

It is hoped that the changing attitude of the medical practitioners will relieve the older person of some of his feelings of uncertainty in dealing with his physician. As the older person feels that his physician regards him as a person and that his needs are not eclipsed by the fact that he is old, it will create a better relationship between them and thus improve the medical care the older person receives.

In all our dealings with illness among the elderly it is of primary importance to keep in mind that illness, and particularly prolonged illness, which so often afflicts the elderly, is not an isolated phenomenon but is often closely related to the patient's economic condition. As someone once said, "the sick are poor and the poor are sick." Or, as Dr. E. M. Bluestone has pointed out on many occasions, illness and poverty form a vicious circle. He says: "The longer a person is sick, the more do neglected social factors impinge themselves on our minds. . . . The poorer the patient, the greater the likelihood that his illness will take a chronic form." [4] This combination of illness and poverty creates a humiliating experience for the individual.

Legislative Action

The awareness of the need for better medical care for the ever increasing number of older people in the community and their difficulty in meeting the cost of care led to the enactment of legislation for Medical Assistance for the Aged. This enabled the older person to secure some form of medical care, providing for doctor's services and meeting the cost of prescriptions. The act was burdened, however, by a number of restrictions, not the least of which was the enforcement of the "means test."

As the deficiencies of this program became more clearly recognized, there was community pressure for the passage of more adequate legislation, which culminated in 1965 in the amendments to the Social Security Act under title XVIII and XIX, popularly known as Medicare and Medicaid respectively.

The Medicare program was designed to provide a wide

[4] Bluestone, "Medical Social Service—a Physican-Administrator's Confession of Faith," p. 56.

range of services to the elderly regardless of their financial situation, thus eliminating the undesirable features of the means test and assuring the older person that he is entitled to medical care as a right.

Medicaid, on the other hand, was meant to defray medical expenses for those not covered under the prepaid medical insurance program, known as Part B of Medicare, and who could not meet the cost through their meager resources, as well as for those who, having exhausted their Medicare benefits, were still in need of medical help. The Medicaid program, however, was not applicable under the act to all localities, and its adoption, or nonadoption, was left to the individual states.

Both Medicare and Medicaid achieved acceptance within a very short time, for they provided what was called many years ago by Dr. I. M. Rubinow "one of the most important factors for decreasing human misery and, by the same token, for increasing human satisfaction."[5] It took some fifty years to change what he called "a hope, an aspiration" into a reality.

A great deal has been written about the inadequate coverage provided by Medicare. For instance, it excludes many items, such as drugs, eye and dental care, as well as other needs so important to the elderly. In addition, the deductible has been increased since the program went into effect, thus increasing the cost of coverage. As a result, the program meets less than half of the average cost for the older person and leaves many problems unsolved. The benefits under Medicare are often exhausted, and supplementation through Medicaid is not always available. Even these avowed shortcomings cannot detract from the important service rendered by Medicare in relieving many elderly of a substantial part of the burden which illness imposes.

[5] Rubinow, "Quest for Security," Preface, p. iii.

To gain an understanding of what Medicare has accomplished let us look at the first annual report on Medicare issued by Wilbur J. Cohen, then Secretary of Health, Education, and Welfare, which was published in 1968 and covered the period from July 1, 1966, through June 30, 1967. It also included some figures for the period up to April, 1968, as a supplement to the report.

The report shows that as of April 1, 1968, the number of elderly enrolled for hospital insurance, Part A of the program, was 19,400,000, while those enrolled in the prepaid medical insurance program (Part B) numbered 18,600,000. Thus, by far the largest proportion of elderly people were entitled to receive the protection available under Medicare.

During the first year of operation, older people received 15 percent to 20 percent more inpatient hospital services than was the case prior to enactment of the Medicare program, and they received these services as private rather than as "charity" patients. The services were rendered by a total of 6,847 (97 percent) of the short-term general hospitals, 4,510 extended care facilities, 2,036 home health agencies, and 2,490 independent laboratories.

The benefits paid under the program from its inception to April, 1968, amounted to $5 billion for hospital insurance and $1 billion for medical insurance.

Impressive as these figures are, it is important to consider those values which cannot be presented in the form of statistics. As the report states:

The lives of many elderly people have been improved and often prolonged by these services. All older people have the security that comes from knowing that serious illness is much less likely to be a major financial problem for them or require them to seek financial help from their children. . . . Another accomplishment . . . was the upgrading of health care that took place as a result of the quality standards established.[6]

President Lyndon B. Johnson commented on the report as follows:

The success of the Medicare Program in its first year has surpassed even the expectations of some of its staunchest supporters. The program is fulfilling the promise that older Americans and their families will be free of major financial hardships because of illness.

Secretary of Health, Education, and Welfare, Wilbur J. Cohen, while endorsing the impressive accomplishments of Medicare, states in his letter of submittal: "It should be noted that Medicare is and will continue to be affected by the basic problems of our health care system, such as shortage of health manpower and facilities and the rising cost of hospital and medical care."

THE RECIPIENTS' RESPONSE TO MEDICARE

The amounts of benefits paid under Medicare show clearly that a considerable number of the elderly took advantage of the program. In addition, independent studies prove that the older people react to Medicare in a positive, accepting way, just as they reacted to social security. In both instances, they appreciate the fact that the benefits come to them as a matter of right, not as charity, and are meant for all older people without regard to their economic status.

In many instances, particularly when the illness is prolonged, they appreciate the fact that thanks to Medicare they are no longer compelled to seek help from their children or from a charitable organization. Despite this accepting attitude, they are discouraged by the fact that Medicare does not pro-

[6] First Annual Report on Medicare," p. 7.

vide the coverage they were led to expect. In addition, difficulties are sometimes encountered because some physicians,
dissatisfied with the inadequate allowances and resentful of the
amount of paperwork required, at times refuse to accept
Medicare patients.

It is of interest to note that in a study conducted among the
elderly in five Midwestern communities, it was found that the
reaction to Medicare differed with the social status of those
questioned. Those with the least knowledge and understanding
of the philosophy of the program were less accepting of it than
were those who were better informed.[7]

INADEQUACIES OF MEDICAID

Medicaid does not share the acceptance and approval granted
to Medicare. Dr. John Knowles, director of the Massachusetts
General Hospital, testifying before a Congressional advisory
committee called Medicaid:

a poor program with no standards, no quality controls, implemented largely by state welfare departments overworked, under-
staffed, and unable to plan medical aspects of programs; per-
petuating the very costly, highly insufficient, inhuman and un-
dignified means tests in the stale atmosphere of charity medicine
carried out in many instances by marginal practitioners in marginal facilities.

Going one step further in an attempt to insure all-inclusive
provisions of medical care of the aged, this Congressional advisory committee, in a report submitted to the U.S. Special
Committee on Aging, included a recommendation for a "comprehensive compulsory health insurance program for all age
groups—a program with built-in cost controls." [8] This is still
considered to be a very controversial proposal, and the likeli-

[7] Coe *et al.*, p. 276.   [8] Knowles, p. 30.

hood of its being adopted in the immediate future is slim. Nevertheless, the very fact that it is being proposed attests to the recognition of the need for adequate medical care for the entire population, as acknowledgment that such care is now not available. It is a forerunner of increasing pressure in that direction in the near future.

Emphasis on Prevention

In any discussion concerning the urgency for medical care, it is essential to keep in mind the importance of preventive measures to insure against the onset of illness.

The attitude that illness among the elderly was due to the very process of aging influenced the thinking of the medical profession and prejudiced them against instituting preventive measures, since obviously old age could not be prevented. Our present-day understanding that age alone is not the only or even the most important factor in determining the need for medical procedures led to acceptance that both treatment and prevention of illness among the elderly should be given the same consideration as is being given in the care of younger patients.

As a result of this changed attitude, we see that the principles of preventive medicine advocated by the U.S. Public Health Service, which have proved successful in dealing with maternal and child health as well as with the treatment of communicable diseases, are now beginning to be applied to the elderly. Efforts are being directed toward the early detection of heart disease, high blood pressure, and possible stroke. The Senate Appropriation committee, recognizing the importance of such efforts, earmarked a special fund for a five-year, comprehensive, nationwide attack on hypertension. Based on the testimony of expert witnesses that "it is possible to control high blood pressure in fifty percent of Americans," the committee concluded that "1.4 million American lives could be saved over the next five years by adequate hypertensive therapy." The report stresses that "what is needed are several pilot studies involving a total community public health effort to uncover high blood pressure among the general public and then to institute effective therapy." [9]

We now see the establishment of special clinics for multiphasic screening under a variety of auspices, such as apartment houses designed as living quarters for the elderly, the objective being the early detection of pathological conditions and access to necessary treatment at the earliest possible moment.

All these developments attest to the increased appreciation of the extensive medical requirements of the aged and of the urgent need to provide adequate care for them. These developments attempt to approximate the concern for the health needs of this particular group—so long neglected—with the efforts which until now have been directed almost exclusively to the younger generation.

As we review the development of medical services for the various groups in our population, we cannot escape the conclusion that in the past the age of the patient played an important role: the younger the patient, the more medical attention he received; conversely, the older the patient, the less attention was directed to him. The beginning change in this attitude, as is being demonstrated in the application of preventive measures and the greater willingness on the part of the medical profession to concentrate on the needs of the elderly,

[9] "Multiphasic Screening Procedures Stressed in Federal Health Programs," p. 34.

augur well for better medical care in the future. We can hope that in the not too distant future neither the age of the patient nor the stage of his illness will blind the medical profession to the person who labors under this double handicap.

ADEQUATE NUTRITION AS A PREVENTIVE MEASURE

Within recent years our attention has been drawn forcibly to the important part which adequate nutrition plays in the maintenance of health in the elderly person. While there is a scarcity of research in this area, estimates indicate that there are as many as eight million older individuals who are undernourished. These figures were derived from the hospitalized older people as well from the experience of agencies which provide hot meals in communal dining rooms, schools, and churches, or deliver them to the homebound. Since we have no information on the total number of older people in the community, or of their state of health, it is possible that the figure cited is in reality an underestimate.

Malnutrition among the elderly may be due to a variety of causes. It may be the result of a lifelong poor eating pattern or the result of illness. At times, it may be the cause of illness. The most important factor, however, is the poverty of millions of elderly people who cannot afford to purchase the kind of food which would supply adequate nutrition.

It was found through experience that insuring a prepared meal is a helpful tool in combating malnutrition. Increase in this service, as well as education as to what constitutes healthy nutritional habits, is essential for many of the elderly. More important, however, is the recognition that an adequate income will go a long way toward improving nutrition among many of the elderly.

The importance of nutrition was underscored at a conference devoted to consideration of the Extension of Human Life Span. It was pointed out that "there appears to be little reason to doubt that the judicious use and development of dietary supplements and restriction of caloric intake to optimum levels will add significantly (e.g. 5–10 years) to healthy life-expectancy." [10]

The panel on aging of the 1969 White House Conference on Food, Nutrition, and Health outlined a number of measures which are essential to combat malnutrition among the elderly. Among the suggestions were: a revision of the food stamp program to meet the needs of larger numbers of older people; surveys of the aged population to discover pathological conditions due to poor diet; inclusion of meal services in all housing programs for the elderly; increased social security benefits and a revision of the public welfare system; development of new lines of food products with adequate nutritional content as well as ease of preparation. It was also recommended to the 1971 White House Conference on Aging that "a review and evaluation of progress in each of these areas be undertaken by a panel on nutrition." [11]

As one reviews these suggestions, the importance of proper nutrition assumes paramount significance. At the same time, one becomes more convinced than ever that the attack on this problem, if it is to be successful, must be many-faceted.

Posthospital Care

Neither preventive measures, important as they are in helping to detect early indications of possible malfunctioning, nor

[10] Strehler, p. 9.
[11] "White House Conference Urges Nutritional Aids for the Elderly," p. 19.

proper hospital care to cure, if possible, or arrest when complete cure cannot be achieved, is the total answer to insure proper medical care in all instances.

Preventive measures are comparatively new as applied to the elderly. On the other hand, the hospital has long been recognized as the primary facility for the care of the sick, including the elderly. This still remains true where the illness requires the highly specialized and centralized equipment of the modern hospital. However, when the illness is prolonged, as is often the case where the elderly are concerned, there may come a time when continued hospitalization, long after the acute episode is over, is not only not helpful, but may be actually detrimental to the older person's physical and mental well-being.

In the past, a great deal of effort has been put into educating the public to the importance of hospital care in case of illness. As a result, the feeling persists in many quarters that "a sick person belongs in a hospital." It is not surprising, therefore, to find that when a recommendation for the patient's discharge is made, even though he shows little or no improvement, it is met with consternation by the patient and frequently by considerable resistance on the part of the family.

Into this resistance goes the family's feeling that perhaps other forms of treatment could have been tried successfully if the patient had remained in the hospital longer. Even more important, however, is the family's fear of taking a sick person into the home. Frequently, this fear is not expressed because of society's disapproval of such an attitude. At other times, however, family members say openly that they are afraid to take a sick elderly person into the home. They are fearful of the burden this would impose and are not sure that they would be able to carry it. They fear that they would be unable to provide the care the patient needs, or meet an emergency, or face the dire consequences should they fail to secure medical help when needed.

The sick person shares the family's feeling of frustrated hope. He is acutely aware, in most instances, of the family's fears and misgivings, even when these are suppressed. Under these circumstances, he cannot help but feel that he is unwelcome in what he considered to be his home.

The hospitals too are caught in a very difficult predicament. While distressed by the inability to help, they nevertheless act on the conviction that prolonged hospitalization of a sick elderly person is inadvisable. Furthermore, because of the large number of elderly sick, they envision that there would soon be a lack of beds if they were to keep people in the hospital without being able to help them in any way. Not only would the facilities be inadequate to care for all the sick elderly, but the hospitals would also be confronted with the situation of being unable to admit patients for whom hospital care is essential. In fact, it has been predicted that by 1980 it will be necessary to double or triple the number of beds available at present. Added to this is the fact that this would demand an increase in professional personnel, which is even now in short supply.

Recognizing the difficulties facing families and hospitals, as well as the need for different forms of treatment at different stages of illness, Medicare incorporated into its program services designed to provide the elderly patient with the kind of care he requires at the particular stage of his illness and to facilitate his gradual adjustment to a return to his family and the community. These services are known as extended care facilities and home care.

EXTENDED CARE FACILITIES

The extended care facilities represent a development of the existing nursing homes. To meet the requirements of the Medicare program the nursing homes designated as extended care facilities are expected to be equipped to render a wide variety of professional services which were heretofore lacking.

Because extended care facilities are part of the total program of medical care, they are required to provide whatever specific treatment is outlined by the referring hospital. Even though "rehabilitation" in the usual sense of the word may be impossible to achieve, the treatment administered in the extended care facility is expected to aim toward eventual restoration to normal living. While it is true that some facilities fall short of this goal, this in no way changes the nature and desirability of the goal itself.

A number of difficulties arise in the attempt to provide adequate facilities for extended care. The amount of money paid by the Medicare program for the service is sometimes unacceptable by the better nursing homes which qualify under this designation. Others do not wish to seek certification under this program as they are unable to provide the needed services because of a shortage of nurses. Another important drawback is the limitation imposed by Medicare on the length of stay in an extended care facility. This means that the patient may have to be discharged, even though his condition may necessitate further care, unless he can pay for a further stay from his own resources.

So far as the patient is concerned, he views admission to the extended care facility as part of his total treatment, since such admission can only be arranged following hospital care.

Consequently, both he and his family accept it willingly, in most instances, viewing it as a step toward his early return home.

The statement has been made that "Extended Care was established as post-hospital care to free hospital beds." [12] It is true that hospital beds are in short supply and that frequently they are occupied by patients suffering from long-term illnesses who cannot use and do not require the extensive facilities which a modern hospital can provide, and that extended care facilities help to free some of these beds. Nevertheless, to cite "to free hospital beds" as the objective of extended care facilities, as if this were the underlying reason for their establishment, not only is inaccurate, but ignores the humane interest of the Medicare program, namely, the desire to provide the type of care which the patient needs and can use to best advantage at a particular period of his illness. This, in effect, is the guiding principle of good medical care on which the Medicare program is based.

HOME CARE

It has been argued that there are not enough hospital beds either in hospitals or in extended care facilities to accommodate all those who need such care. Furthermore, construction of additional medical facilities would not solve the problem because there is a shortage of personnel. Perhaps what is needed is not so much additional institutional beds, but the willingness to use to advantage the beds in the older persons' own homes.

The present-day trend not to confine patients to institutions is well-established. It is justified on several grounds.

[12] Gosette, p. 1.

Economically, the cost of institutional care is high. What is equally important is that it is more and more recognized that prolonged institutionalization or hospitalization is detrimental to the older person's welfare. In addition, it is well known that people are happier in their own home with their families if this can be arranged.

In view of these advantages, a coordinated home care program was established at the Montefiore Hospital in New York City. The first of its kind, it offers a variety of medical, nursing, and social work services; in fact, it represents an extension of the hospital into the community, furnishing all necessary services without confining the person to a hospital bed.

Experience with coordinated programs of home care have demonstrated that care in the patient's home is a valuable alternative to care in an institution and that, in fact, the sick person profits by such care. The very fact that he is in familiar surroundings, that he has the care and attention of those closest to him, that when the doctor visits, the patient has his undivided attention—all are conducive to a more favorable response to the care he receives.

In addition, family members, assured of comprehensive care and of a quick response to their call for help, are able to overcome their resistance to the sick patient's discharge from the hospital. The success of the program led to its adoption in many hospitals throughout the country and served as a model when the home care program under Medicare was organized.

While the establishment of the home care program was based on the need to give the sick person the care needed at the moment, it was found that it provided another important service. It enabled the older person not only to face discharge from the hospital with the assurance that his medical needs would be cared for, but it enabled him to remain a part of the family group. The fact that family members are actively involved in his care and are willing to tend to his needs assures the patient of their interest and concern and helps to strengthen family ties.

Mental Health of the Elderly

Advanced age often brings with it a deterioration of mental health. Unfortunately, the neglect of ailments among the elderly has been even more pronounced where mental ill-health was concerned. As a result, we find that there has been less understanding of mental disorders among the elderly and less ability—or even inclination—to study its causes or to institute treatment procedures than was the situation in the case of physical ill-health. Here too, it was assumed that mental illness was part of the process of aging and that therefore it predetermined an unfavorable prognosis and consequently underlined the uselessness of attempts at treatment. The elderly mentally disturbed patients frequently found their way to mental hospitals, where they remained indefinitely, forgotten and untreated, with a consequent further deterioration in the majority of cases.

There is evidence that within recent years, concomitant with a general increase of interest in mental health, the attitude toward mental illness among the aged has shown a significant change.

The medical profession is now recognizing that deterioration of mental health and behavior disorders are not always —and in fact need not be—part of the aging process. It is now accepted by many physicians that a variety of factors may be responsible for the symptoms of disorder manifested by the elderly. Such symptoms as withdrawal, forgetfulness, and temporary confusion may be due to intolerable social situations. One might cite such precipitating factors as bereavement, loneliness, economic insecurity or insecurity in any other area, despair, loss of self-esteem, loss of social status and prestige, loss of hope—all of these, so frequently seen among the elderly, may create feelings of worthlessness, frustration, and loss of a significant role and purpose in life.

Serious physical illnesses too may give rise to a variety of mental symptoms which disappear if and when the physical condition is treated successfully. It is important to keep in mind also that the neurotic tendencies and unhealthy personality patterns which the elderly person may manifest can be a carry-over from his earlier years and may become aggravated as the individual is faced with the numerous deprivations so often imposed by aging.

As a result of this better understanding of the causes which frequently underlie disturbed behavior, physicians no longer regard its manifestations as irreversible or untreatable. Custodial care in mental institutions is now not only seen to be inadequate and failing to meet the needs of the elderly, but is recognized as being wasteful both economically and in terms of human happiness.

It is believed that many of the elderly could be removed from the unfavorable institutional environment and treated successfully in the community.

Experience has demonstrated that in some instances elderly patients who are suffering from a mild mental disorder can adjust in a satisfactory manner in a general institution for the care of the aged, provided the atmosphere is geared to accepting their particular manifestations, is nonthreatening, and the treatment is compatible with the requirements of their mental state.

As an illustration of the beneficial effects of such an atmosphere one can cite the experience of the Jewish Home and Hospital for the Aged in New York. This institution admitted some of the elderly patients who were ready for discharge from a mental hospital but who had no home to which to return and needed some supervision. They were placed in the institution together with other elderly individuals. The atmosphere was relaxed, undemanding, and they were treated with understanding and concern. Many of these patients were able to make an adjustment which was considered "good" in some instances and "satisfactory" in others.

That attention to his needs and evidence of concern can be beneficial to the older person's welfare even when no change can be effected in his mental condition is illustrated by Mrs. Miller:

Mrs. Miller, a 70-year-old woman, was living alone in a hotel for older citizens. She was referred to an agency by the landlord because of the dirty condition of her room and person.

Mrs. Miller was found to be living in a room which was crowded to the ceiling with all sorts of papers and debris. Mrs. Miller herself was covered with scabs as a result of long accumulation of dirt. An unpleasant odor emanated from her unwashed body.

Although she was able to sustain a conversation and arrange for the payment of her rent every month by selling one of her holdings, she showed no understanding of her need for help, nor of the community facilities which might be available to her.

Because no one was willing to assume the responsibility of declaring her incompetent, arrangements were made to secure a housekeeper who was willing to go in and help clean up the room, even though she had to work with gloves and a mask. Securing additional help, the housekeeper was able to give Mrs. Miller a bath. Underneath her scabs, there were open wounds which required medical attention.

As Mrs. Miller looked at her hands after the bath, she exclaimed, "I am clean!"

Arrangements were made to provide the necessary medical help; secure professional advice in arranging her financial affairs, and have her admitted to a home for the aged where she could receive proper supervision.

A report from the home for the aged indicated that she was adjusting well and was pleased about the care she was receiving.

Acting on the conviction that some of the mildly disturbed elderly do not need the environment of a mental institution, the provisions of the Medicare program were utilized to give a number of institutionalized patients a different and more satisfactory type of care. These patients were discharged from the mental hospitals to nursing homes, their care there being paid for through Medicare funds. While the atmosphere in these nursing homes is undeniably pleasanter than that in state mental hospitals, it has not yet been determined whether the transfer benefited the patients' mental condition. This would depend primarily on the type of care and attention the nursing homes are able and willing to make available.

A THERAPEUTIC COMMUNITY

A striking illustration of a different way of helping the mentally ill to achieve a satisfactory adjustment is presented by a program of care in Geel, Belgium.

A visitor to that community in 1968 found that 1,890 patients were being cared for in what was called "the colony." Some were confined in a small central infirmary, but the majority lived in foster homes. Approximately one family out of six had in its care one or two "more or less severely impaired, predominantly chronic mental patients, who otherwise would have been locked up in an institution, perhaps for life." One third of the patients suffered from "functional disorders, largely psychotic"; the rest were mentally retarded.

Those who resided with families were treated as boarders. They shared the family's daily food, work, social and recreational activities. They could attend community functions, go to the church, movies, sports events. Wide allowances were made for them not only by the families with whom they resided, but by the community at large. Any manifestations of peculiar behavior were generally disregarded. The acceptance of these patients is part of the tradition of the community.

This originated in the fifteenth century, at a time when the mentally ill were usually regarded as witches and tortured. At first, placement of patients in the homes was arranged on a family-to-family basis. Gradually, the program shifted first to the control of the municipal government, later to the federal government, and in 1948 it was placed under the jurisdiction of the National Ministry of Health. The government pays for the care of all but a small number (about 10 percent) of the patients. The others are able to meet their own expenses. Demand for this type of care exceeds the supply, and there is a waiting list.

Medical facilities are limited. A visiting physician makes a periodic inspection of the homes and at that time examines and treats any physical complaints which are brought to his attention. Behavior problems are also discussed during these visits. Psychiatric treatment is not available, and in general treatment is custodial in nature. Because the families accept the adult patient as if he were a grown-up child, there is little opportunity for him to achieve a higher level of functioning.

The author of the article on the Geel program ascribes the satisfactory adjustment of these patients to the fact that the environment is that of a supportive family "where the patient is accepted for what he is, not rejected because he is not what he should be." This attitude, despite the custodial nature of treatment, impedes the deterioration that occurs so often among patients who remain in mental hospitals for long periods of time.

Though the program was not designed for, nor does it emphasize the care of, elderly mental patients, nevertheless it has important implications for this particular group. In fact, some elderly, mentally ill patients were included in the total number cared for in the foster family plan, so that the general findings apply to them in the same way that they apply to other age groups. Some of the families expressed their preference for older patients. This would seem to indicate that those elderly patients who were placed in the community in the past had made a satisfactory adjustment.

As a result of his visit to the colony, the writer came to the conclusion that this community has "demonstrated the potentials of spontaneous therapy latent in the lay community." He states that "it remains to be seen whether such a program, supplemented by modern therapeutic techniques, can outlive the current threats of industrialization and urbanization." [13]

A study to examine the potentials inherent in this program

[13] "Visit to the 500-Year-old Prototype of the Therapeutic Community," pp. 2–3.

is being conducted by the Columbia University Faculty of Medicine, the New York State Psychiatric Institute, and the University of Louvain, Belgium. Dr. Leo Srole, Director of the project, prepared a progress report when the study was in the third year of operation, outlining the purpose, scope, and tentative findings of this international, interuniversity, and interdisciplinary undertaking.

The report states that it contains "more extensive and intensive exploration of a sizeable universe of families than has hitherto been reported in the literature of the social sciences" and that it presents "a lay milieu therapy in a pure and advanced form."

As outlined, the purpose of the study is to determine whether the conditions under which the family foster care program operates might be a "viable alternative to hospitalization in other kinds of settings." Recognizing that so far it is not known how the program works or the reason for its success, an attempt will be made to analyze the factors in the patient and in the foster family which have an effect on the success or failure of the experiment, on the residents in care, on the past residents, and on the foster families." An effort will also be made to test the hypothesis that "the degree to which the patient is integrated or 'incorporated' into the family structure, in roles changing from extremes of a transient-boarder to a *de facto* kinsman is predictive of his changes."

The interim conclusion is that the study of the Geel program

gives promise of enlarging our basic knowledge and of contributing to the care of the large segment . . . of the chronically disabled for whom psychiatric hospitalization is unnecessary. [The report points out that] comparison of patients in Geel foster families and Belgium's traditional mental hospitals highlights the contrasting consequences of freedom and sequestration. . . . The comparison of such cases suggests that Geel prevents regression into social breakdown syndromes associated with custodial institutions and . . . stimulates a higher level of functioning. [A study of these factors would] justify refinement and reapplication.[14]

When the final results of this study are made available, they may indeed prove to be of great significance in determining the advisability of instituting similar programs elsewhere. This would go a long way in providing more adequate help for the mentally ill elderly than is now available in facilities for their care.

Since such new and far-reaching programs are still in the distant future, it is important that in the meantime we gain a better appreciation of the meaning of illness, whether physical or mental, to the older individual himself as well as to the members of his family, and of its effect on the relationship between them.

Effect of Illness on the Individual

In most instances, advanced age sooner or later brings with it a variety of illnesses. Long before a serious illness strikes, the older person may become aware of minor changes in his physical well-being, of decreased strength, frequent fatigue, loss of energy, minor aches and pains which come and go. He may become subject to periods of temporary disorientation, or of occasional losses of memory. At first, he may attempt to negate the seriousness of these minor

[14] Srole, "Progress Report on Geel Foster Family Care Research Project." p. 3.

manifestations. However, their recurrence at more and more frequent intervals creates fear and apprehension.

There comes a time when a serious illness brings with it not only discomfort and pain, but discouragement and anxiety as to the eventual outcome. The older person finds that he can no longer brush it aside as being but a temporary indisposition for it persists and becomes aggravated. While it is true that persons of any age can, and do, become afflicted with serious illness which can give rise to similar reactions, nevertheless the younger man can take courage and hope as he witnesses his gradual response to medical attention and treatment; not so the elderly, whose diminishing recuperative powers respond more slowly, if at all, to the doctor's ministrations, and who sees himself becoming more incapacitated and weaker as time goes on, despite all the efforts of his physician. Finally, there comes a time when he cannot escape the conclusion that medical skill is helpless to ease his suffering, and that he must accept the inexorable progress of his illness.

We are only now beginning to question the physical and mental effects of illness, and particularly of prolonged illness, on the elderly person. What happens to such a person when he is confined to a so-called "geriatric ward", the very name of which connotes hopelessness? Or when he is transferred from the general hospital, to which he was originally admitted, to a hospital for chronic diseases? It does not require great acuity or medical knowledge for him to realize that the move indicates a worsening of his condition.

There can be no definitive answers to these questions. Any discussion brings us face-to-face with the old truism that in all situations, individuals differ, and, their responses are determined by background, previous experiences and their goals and aspirations. All these factors will influence the reaction of the older person as the realization is forced upon him that his illness is not responding to treatment, that apparently it cannot be helped by existing medical knowledge and skill, that hope for recovery is dwindling, and that for him, time is indeed running out.

In the variety of responses to prolonged illness, its problems, and its outcome, two factors occur with such frequency as to be almost universal: (1) the importance of the physician's interest and the meaning to the patient when this interest is diminished or totally withdrawn, and (2) the dependence so frequently imposed by illness, and its meaning to the patient. Let us consider these factors in greater detail, for they deserve special attention.

IMPORTANCE OF THE DOCTOR'S INTEREST

The most important element in facilitating the older patient's adjustment to prolonged hospitalization and the demands of his illness is his ongoing relationship with his physician. The sick man may resent his need to depend on others for the satisfaction of his everyday needs. So far as his physician is concerned, however, the patient not only does not resent his dependence, but actually looks for it and accepts it gratefully.

The aged patient seeks help from his doctor both for the alleviation of troublesome physical symptoms and for interest in, and understanding of, the numerous problems which come with illness. This is not always easy to come by, for it demands from the physician an extra measure of patience and investment of a considerable amount of time. When the busy doctor is unable, or at times unwilling, to involve himself in the patient's problems, the latter feels that he is rejected and neglected by the person on whom he counted for help.

Unfortunately, the very fact that the patient shows little or no improvement as a result of treatment may evoke an unfavorable response from the physician. The latter, feeling that despite his best efforts he is unable to better the patient's condition, and convinced of the hopelessness of the task, succumbs to a feeling of futility and solves it by removing himself; he simply ceases to care for the sick man. Such removal of the professional interest deprives the patient not only of the possible advantage of appropriate medical treatment, such as attention to any intercurrent illness, but also of the invaluable comfort and hope which manifestation of interest and concern can instill.

The patient is often only too clearly aware of the meaning of such neglect. He becomes convinced that the doctor's changed attitude is due to the fact that there is nothing more he can do. The break in the professional relationship confirms his suspicion that his condition is hopeless, and this intensifies his fear of impending death. Even though, admittedly, the help which the physician can give may be minimal, nevertheless an attempt to institute some simple palliative measures can be of inestimable value in lessening the physical discomfort and the apprehension it inspires.

Fortunately, the former helplessness on the part of a physician confronted with a prolonged illness in an elderly patient is slowly giving way to an understanding that illnesses of the elderly are not always irreversible or untreatable. This, in turn, inspires a greater readiness to take the necessary steps toward helping the patient's physical and emotional problems.

DEPENDENCE IMPOSED BY ILLNESS

A certain amount of dependency is often manifested during illness. It becomes even more evident when the illness necessitates admission to a hospital. In fact, the very rendering of essential medical treatment demands a dependent role; unless it is accepted, it may seriously interfere with the patient's response to treatment.

The way in which the elderly patient reacts to the loss of personal security and to the need to become dependent on others will be conditioned by the same factors which were responsible for his ability or inability to accept—or even seek—dependence when confronted with economic insufficiency, namely, by the extent to which his dependency needs have been satisfied or thwarted in the past.

For those persons who need to satisfy a previously unattainable dependence, illness and incapacity provide an acceptable, socially sanctioned way to do so. Thus some patients accept the dependency necessitated by their illness with resignation and a willing compliance. They appear grateful for anything that is done for them; they do what the hospital personnel expect them to do; they "give no trouble," and they are rewarded by being given praise and attention.

On the other hand, those patients who cherish their independence and who are filled with anxiety, fear, and despair when they must give it up often reject the help offered them and insist on doing things for themselves despite serious limitations and the pain which such activities often entail. They may even feel that their helpless state and the attention which others give them are proof of their personal inadequacy. They complain: "I am not normal. There is some-

thing wrong with me if others have to do for me what I
should be doing for myself."

When no longer able to maintain even this amount of
independence, these patients may vent their frustrations by
becoming dissatisfied, exacting, imposing on others, as if to
demonstrate their ability to maintain control over the situation in which they find themselves. The complexity and
variety of the needs underlying and influencing such patients'
behavior will demand from all concerned with their care and
wishing to be of help to them an amount of understanding
and tolerance which is not always possible for hospital
personnel to achieve.

Effect of Physical Illness on Family Relationships

As was to be expected, the effect of the older person's illness
differs in different circumstances, and, as in many other instances, it is seriously influenced by the relationship which
existed prior to the time when the patient became ill. Whatever the effect in any situation may be, there is little doubt
that the illness and incapacity of an elderly person involve
members of the family. The involvement may be characterized by genuine interest, concern, and a willingness to
be helpful no matter how difficult the situation may be. In
other instances, such devotion, concern, and helpfulness are
lacking, which produces serious detrimental effects on the
sick elderly person as well as on his adjustment to the illness
and his incapacity.

Difficulties are created for both the sick person and
members of his family when the elderly individual is suffering from a prolonged illness, and when his long sojourn in

a hospital puts special stress on all those concerned with his welfare. Too often, as the illness progresses, as the hospital stay lengthens, and the patient's condition continues to deteriorate, family members, feeling helpless and uncomfortable because of their helplessness, tend to visit more rarely. Deprived of the beneficial effects of the continued interest of the physician, to whom he looked for help, the patient's feeling of having been abandoned is aggravated by the apparent loss of his family's interest in him. No one can doubt that this removal of interest by all significant persons in his environment often has a detrimental effect and undermines the patient's readiness to fight the progress of his illness.

PARENTS' RELATIONSHIP TO CHILDREN

The dependence of the older sick person may be particularly difficult for him to accept when it means dependence on his children. Such dependence, which often includes accepting help with his daily needs, creates a reversal of roles and threatens the maintenance of accustomed relationships. The older person may fear that he will lose the respect of his children as well as his role in the family. While at times these feelings may result in the parent's refusal to accept help, in other instances, in an effort to maintain his authority and to assert his worth, the parent may demand even more attention and love.

This increased need for attention and concern is particularly apparent when the elderly person is attempting to make the difficult adjustment to the strange environment of the hospital. All those who work in a hospital as well as those who have ever been hospitalized know only too well the impatience with which the patients await the daily mail and visiting hours, and the anticipation with which they watch the door for the appearance of their visitors. To them, this represents the highlight of the hospital day. The more prolonged the illness and the longer the hospitalization, the more important becomes this show of interest on the part of family members and friends. Unfortunately, too often visits decrease in frequency, and the elderly sick person is left with the conviction that he has been abandoned by those closest to him. It is not surprising that he succumbs to a feeling of hopelessness.

The feeling of being abandoned often produces not only hopelessness and irritation, but at times even a feeling of guilt, as the older person begins to question what he may have done to forfeit their interest. On the other hand, their continued interest may indicate to him that he had performed his role as a parent satisfactorily. There was Mr. Black, for instance:

> Mr. Black was suffering from Buerger's disease and had to endure severe pain. Several amputations had kept him in the hospital for a long period of time.
>
> His wife and children continued their frequent visits and tried to show their love and concern in many ways.
>
> In the midst of all his suffering, Mr. Black frequently reverted to a recital of his past life. He emphasized the fact that he was a good husband and father. The attention he was receiving now that he was sick and helpless was proof, he said, that he performed his duties well and deserved the devotion now shown him.

CHILDREN'S RELATIONSHIP TO PARENTS

The statement is often heard that children are indifferent to their parents' illness, and even resentful of the burden which such illness imposes on them. While one can cite instances where this attitude is shown, in reality such a negative attitude is apparent only in isolated cases. In most instances, children show concern for their ailing parent and a desire to be as helpful as they can possibly be. What is significant is the fact that such concern is often demonstrated even where the relationship had not been a close one. It is possible that in such instances the children may attempt to atone for past neglect. Whatever the motivation may be, it appears that few can remain indifferent to illness and suffering.

Even in those instances where the relationship in the past was a close and affectionate one—or perhaps because of it—children may remove themselves from the situation because they cannot endure to witness the severe pain, suffering, and progressive deterioration of their parent. Their very involvement with the patient and their reaction to his illness may interfere with their continuing ability to provide the emotional support which the patient needs. This may precipitate their withdrawal from active participation in his care and may be misinterpreted as indicative of indifference. Mr. Kane's story as he told it to the agency worker, when he applied for nursing home care for his father, is eloquent testimony of the burden of pain which illness frequently brings to family members who are sincerely concerned with a patient's welfare:

Mr. Kane told what it meant to him and to his wife to see his father's gradual deterioration. He spoke of his father as a person who was always strong, "a tower of strength." All the members of the family would turn to him for advice. "It is hard to realize," he said, "that he is so helpless now, and that he needs to depend on others for everything."

They were only too glad to take care of him, but they found that his suffering and increasing inability to care for himself were more than they were able to endure. "Do you realize what it means to face this situation day after day, week after week?" he questioned.

Somehow they had managed until now, but they have come to a point where they can no longer continue. His father, who is mentally alert, himself brought up the possibility of entering a nursing home, for he felt that they had carried a heavy burden for far too long a time.

Throughout this recital, Mr. Kane maintained his composure. As he described in detail the kind of care his father needed and asked for reassurance that the nursing home would provide it, he broke down and cried. "If this is what happens to a person at the end of a productive life, I hope I will not reach old age," he said.

This identification of a middle-aged man with the deterioration which old age often brings is not unusual and is intensified by the genuine concern which he feels for his parent.

Members of the family, as well as the older person himself, are frequently subject to feelings of guilt when they must cope with a serious illness. The children may question their contribution to the predicament in which the older person finds himself. They may ascribe his suffering to their neglect of him in the past, whether or not such neglect really occurs. Frequently they attempt to atone by showing an extra measure of concern. Or, in an attempt to assuage their conscience, adult children may sometimes undertake an economic burden of providing special care which they are in reality not able to carry and which is not necessitated by their parent's condition. At times, when this increased concern represents a sudden change in attitude, one might question how the unusual manifestation of interest affects the older person. It would not be surprising to find that, aware of the change in the attitude of those around him, the older sick person interprets it as an indication of the seriousness of his condition.

The assumption of increased responsibility for their parent's welfare may create for the children a serious dilemma, as they find themselves conflicted as to whether their responsibility to their parent interferes with the adequate discharge of their responsibility to their own children, as was demonstrated in the case of Mr. Green, discussed in Chapter 4.

Not only the children, but the marital partner as well is often assailed by guilt when confronted with a serious illness of the mate. There were Mr. and Mrs. White, for instance:

> Mr. White, a successful businessman, had always provided adequately for the family, and protected his wife from any responsibility. He made all the decisions, and was always there to help her with the handling of the household.
>
> When Mr. White became ill, afflicted by a progressive neurological condition which made it impossible for him to do much for himself, Mrs. White was suddenly confronted with the need to assume full responsibility for herself and for her husband.
>
> Now, she had no one on whom to depend; in addition, she was subjected to constant criticism by her husband. His critical, petulant, unreasonable, and demanding attitude was so different from his previous behavior that she found it difficult to become accustomed to it, even though she understood that it was due to his illness.
>
> What disturbed her most of all was the feeling of overwhelming guilt. As she put it, "He always took care of

me. Now, when he needs me, I cannot take care of him as he would want me to do."

EFFECT OF MENTAL ILLNESS ON FAMILIES

The effect of mental illness, or even a slight deviation from normal, such as temporary confusion, forgetfulness, irritability, or depression, often presents even more difficulties than does a serious physical illness.

Mental illness, regardless of its origin or of the length of time it persist, poses an additional threat to the uninitiated layman. The still prevalent lack of understanding of mental illness, the stigma which clings to it, and the fear of it make it difficult for families to accept it or to cope with its manifestations.

The family doctor, to whom they turn for help under these circumstances, is too often neither willing nor equipped to diagnose and successfully treat a mental patient or to give the family the reassurance and help which would enable them to provide the necessary care. Even when the family doctor makes a referral to a psychiatrist, it often fails to insure that the help they seek will be forthcoming. Psychiatrists, even as the medical profession in general, are often unwilling to devote the necessary time and energy to the problems of the mentally ill elderly, tending to concentrate on treatment of the young.

Faced with the older person's unfamiliar and frightening behavior over prolonged periods of time, or when these manifestations recur frequently, family members, unable to secure the help they need, may have to resort to the only resource open to them, and have the elderly relative admitted to a mental hospital. This step is not an easy one for the family to take. The decision is often arrived at after long soul-searching and against their innermost wishes, but only because they feel that there is nothing else to do.

Even after the step is taken, family members may be besieged by a variety of doubts. They may be fearful of the kind of treatment the patient will receive, or may be apprehensive that such hospitalization may become permanent. Because of society's attitude toward mental illness and mental hospitals, they are often concerned about the reaction of their friends and relatives, who may fail to understand their position and blame them, or even ostracize them, for having "sent their relative away."

As an example of what mental illness can mean to a family, let us consider the case of Mr. and Mrs. Walters:

Mrs. Walters was 64 years old. For the past three years she had been noticing significant changes in her husband, ten years her senior.

At first, he appeared merely forgetful, silent, withdrawn, spending most of his time sitting at the window. While Mrs. Walters felt disturbed about the developing lack of communication between them, and the fact that her husband's behavior confined her to the house, depriving her of all social contacts, she was able to adjust to the situation with minimum resentment.

As time went on, however, Mr. Walters's condition worsened. He became slovenly in his habits, which disgusted his wife. Later, he developed the habit of taking knives to bed with him. Mrs. Walters reacted with fear and misgiving to this new development.

As Mr. Walters's condition continued to deteriorate, Mrs. Walters was finally able to admit that perhaps her husband should not remain at home. She could not consider a mental hospital, however, and spoke about the possibility of a "nursing home." When it was pointed out to her that a doctor would have to decide where Mr. Walters should be admitted, she postponed for a long time before having her husband examined.

When an examination was finally arranged, and the doctor recommended admission to a mental hospital, Mrs. Walters's guilt became overwhelming, and it took considerable time and persuasion on the part of the social worker for her to agree to the plan.

Even when she became convinced that hospitalization was the only answer to the unbearable situation in the home, she found herself under attack by various members of the family. They could not understand that she would agree to such a plan; they frightened her with numerous stories of mistreatment to which her husband would be subjected, and criticized her for the step she was about to take.

As was to be expected, this attitude reactivated and aggravated her feelings of guilt, completely immobilized her, and made it impossible for her to take any action. She required a great deal of support and reassurance before she was able to withstand the criticism of her relatives and proceed with the necessary arrangements to have her husband committed.

While a great deal of her apprehension eased as she was able to see for herself that her husband was not being ill-treated, nevertheless, she found difficulty in freeing herself of the doubts as to whether she had done the right thing and she needed continued help with her feelings of guilt for a prolonged period of time.

There can be little question that the care of a mentally sick relative represents considerable difficulty for his family. This is due partly to the fact that the average layman is unfamiliar with, and threatened by, what are considered to be the "bizarre manifestations" of mental illness which are incomprehensible and frightening to him. Furthermore, the conflicts and attitudes which develop through the many years of living together interfere with the family members' ability to provide proper care without injecting their own emotional reactions. The Geel project demonstrates that some mentally ill patients can be handled adequately by people outside the immediate family group who are not intimately involved with the patient and can accept him without themselves being threatened by his deviant or unacceptable behavior. As the Geel project report indicates, in this situation "the patient starts unencumbered by the conflicts and strains of the malignant kind that have probably been rooted and grown over the years within the natural family." [15]

As our society becomes more complex and the strains on all members and particularly on the elderly, become more severe, the incidence of mental disturbance may be expected to rise. While it is true that elderly mentally ill patients can, in some instances, be cared for more easily by strangers than by kinfolk, it is doubtful whether an arrangement such as exists in Geel would be possible in our highly industrialized culture, even if it were found to be desirable.

Other ways of caring for the elderly mentally ill will have to be devised, but the success of any plan would depend on the better understanding of emotional problems by the patient's family, by the physicians, and by the community at large. There is no gainsaying the fact that the care of the sick elderly often creates a variety of serious difficulties for members of their families. Nevertheless, one cannot close one's eyes to the fact that all too often institutionalization is resorted to without too much thought being given to possible

[15] *Ibid.*

alternatives. In many instances the need for institutionalizing the elderly could be avoided. What is needed is a greater appreciation of the isolation and degradation to which the elderly are often subjected by such treatment and an increased willingness to develop and utilize specialized services.

7. IMPACT OF EXTENDED LEISURE TIME

As OUR DISCUSSION INDICATED, retirement affects not only the economic condition of the older person—he must adjust to an income which may well be substantially below the one to which he had become accustomed, as well as to the need to accept at times an unwelcome dependency. The combination of earlier retirement and prolonged life span also has a profound impact on other aspects of his life. He feels separated from the world of work, and consequently feels that he has lost status and worth. Moreover, often he has more leisure time than he knows how to use. These changes in his mode of living are not only disturbing in themselves, they also influence the way in which the older person relates to the community and to the members of his family.

Feeling of Exclusion

When a man works, the greater part of his day is devoted to the job on hand. Leisure time is welcomed eagerly as a change and a respite from what becomes on occasion a tiresome grind. Unlimited free time, however, often leaves a void which may be difficult to fill. The retired individual must discover how best to utilize the excess of free hours suddenly made available to him and for which he is often ill-prepared. He may find that it is not easy to do.

The free time of the retired person is not a matter of temporary inability to find work, an experience which many working people encounter in the course of a lifetime. The combination of a lengthened life span and a shortened work life brings the need to cope with longer years of inactivity, years during which he is completely separated from the world of work, a world which occupied such an important part of his life.

Not all the elderly feel the same way about this change in their way of life. There are those who look forward to retirement and welcome it as an opportunity for enjoying leisure and participating in activities of interest to them. There are others, however, for whom work was the main interest and who feel lost and useless without it. This feeling is aggravated by the fact that we live in a society which emphasizes the importance of work and productivity as conferring status, and is inclined to disregard both a man's past contribution and the fact that his retirement, while he was still capable of producing, was imposed by society itself. Too often society pushes him aside and acts as if he were no longer able to share common interests and concerns, and the older person is thus thrown more and more into association mostly (or even exclusively) with others of his own age group, restricting his contact with the life around him. This may eventually lead to complete separation from the life of the community and creates what has been called a "sub-culture of the aged."

What the adjustment to retirement may entail is told graphically by James Brown as he relates his experience:

I am 66 years old and until last year I was employed as a bookkeeper in a large firm, where I had been working since I graduated from high school. The work became more interesting as I was advanced and was given additional responsibilities.

As happens to others, once in a while I got tired of the daily routine. Vacations came but once a year, and I found myself wishing for the time when I could quit working, perhaps be able to take an extended trip with my wife. How long should a man work? There comes a time when one should stop working and take it easy. At least, that's what I thought.

The time to stop came last year. I was glad to retire, even though a bit sorry to leave the accustomed surroundings and the many friends among my fellow employees. This feeling, how-ever, soon passed, and I convinced myself that I was not really leaving my friends—I could still see them whenever I wanted to.

I became quite excited about all the fuss that was being made —the farewell luncheon, to which my wife was invited, the speeches, all the nice things said about me by my employer and fellow employees. And, there was the gold watch with the in-scription—a tangible proof that my work was appreciated.

As the luncheon party broke up, my friends came over to wish me luck. Each one in turn reminded me not to forget them, to drop in at the office from time to time and tell them what retirement was really like. After all, they said, they too would be retiring soon.

It was pleasant to be free, to go for a walk when the weather was nice, to read the morning paper leisurely, and to visit friends with my wife. I did drop in a few times at the office to greet my former co-workers with, "Well, slaves, still working?" and to tell them what I had been doing with my free time.

After a while, I found that these visits were not so satisfying as I thought they would be. The people were talking about their work, excited about the changes that were being made, and I felt that I was an outsider. I had nothing to contribute to the discussion, and it made me feel useless.

All the other ways of filling in the empty hours also began to lose their appeal. After all, a vacation is only a vacation when it comes after a period of work, and is doubly appreciated because it is short. A perpetual vacation is no vacation at all, I discovered.

There came a day when I woke up and said to myself: "Well, James Brown, what are you going to do with yourself today?" I could find no answer to this question. Somehow, all the things I was planning to do when I was looking forward to retirement seemed to have disappeared into thin air.

I could look forward only to just another day to kill, watching my wife as she went about her household chores wandering aimlessly in and out of the kitchen, offering to help and being told that there was nothing for me to do—"Just take it easy, relax," my wife advised.

I would leave the house, feeling that I was in the way. I would go for the newspaper the long way so it would consume more time. I would listen to the radio, watch television, and envy people who were busy at their work. I would visit with a neighbor, exchanging a few words about the weather and the news.

Through it all, I found myself becoming less and less interested, I mean really interested in other people and in what was happening around me.

I knew that I could not go on like this, but had no idea what I could do to make me feel useful once again.

My son, who visited quite often, noticed that something was wrong. I no longer talked about how wonderful it was to be free of the work, to do what I wanted. He began to press me with questions. It was a relief to tell someone how I really felt. He wondered whether I would be interested in volunteering some of my free time to a charitable organization with which he was connected, and offer my services as a bookkeeper.

I accepted the suggestion eagerly. Before too long, the feeling of being useful returned. I was meeting new people, made new friends, and felt part of the world of work—I was alive again.

Definitely, retirement is not all it is "cracked up" to be.

Isolation of the Elderly

Mr. Brown's reaction to retirement is not unique. He is not alone in feeling lost when separated from the workaday world. Unfortunately, there are many who face the difficulties of this period without the companionship of a mate or the interest of concerned children.

It is these elderly who have aroused the interest of various groups. Within recent years there have been studies which seek to determine the extent of isolation among the elderly. There appears to be a wide divergence in the interpretation of the findings. For instance, a report given at a meeting of the British Geriatric Society in 1969 indicates that of 89 institutionalized patients studied in the Geriatric Department of St. James Hospital in Leeds, England, only 25 were truly isolated. This finding was supported by the statement that only these 25 patients had "only one or less visits per week." The study concluded that "our impression is that although many old people complain of being lonely, few of them are in fact isolated." [1] Another survey, however found that among 176 elderly people sampled at random, "daily contact is extremely limited . . . as sixty percent of our sample have no daily visit from a child and 91 percent have no daily visit from a relative." [2]

[1] Droller, *Does Community Care Really Reach the Elderly Sick?* p. 174.

[2] Bishop and Manby, p. 1710.

One might justifiably question whether weekly or daily visits are reliable indications of the presence or absence of isolation. Perhaps more important, from the point of view of the older person, is their statement that they "feel lonely." According to Webster's dictionary, "loneliness" carries with it an implication of depression. Thus, what is important is not so much the number of visitors, but the significance of the particular visitor to the elderly person. Furthermore, there are individual variations in the reaction of people to being or not being visited. Some may feel isolated and alone even when surrounded by relatives and friends, while others have little need for personal contacts and may not feel isolated even if they have no visitors.

The extent of the isolation of elderly people in rural areas may be judged from a study undertaken by the National Council on the Aging, in which the following statement appears: "Often the older poor are hard to find. . . . Some are invisible and unknown to everyone in the community, with the possible exception of the postman." [3] Similarly, those living in the high-rise apartment houses of the large cities often do not know their next-door neighbor.

In order to study isolation among the elderly, we would need to establish meaningful criteria to measure it, not in terms of numbers of visits, but of the deeper meaning of loneliness and isolation to the elderly involved.

THE THEORY OF DISENGAGEMENT

Published reports indicate that there is considerable difference of opinion as to what is responsible for such isolation as exists among the elderly. There are those who argue that the isolation is the result of society's attitude; that society ex-

[3] Chandler, p. 9.

cludes and segregates this group and refuses to permit them significant participation in the life of the community. In other words, society in its relations with the elderly utilizes the same approach which it frequently employs in its approach to other groups who are not considered significant in the life of the community. Under these circumstances, it might not be surprising to find that the elderly person, in an attempt to protect himself from further hurt, tends to withdraw. It is as if he were saying: "All right, if you do not want me, I do not need you."

On the other hand, there are those who claim that it is not society which excludes the elderly, but that the older person himself withdraws from contact. The proponents of this point of view have developed the concept known as the "theory of disengagement." To explain the frequent occurrence of alienation among the elderly, the theory advances the propostion that there is an "inevitable mutual withdrawal or disengagement between the aging person and others in the social system to which he belongs." [4] This concept has been elaborated as follows: "The individual prepares for death and tends to disengage. He becomes preoccupied with himself and is less concerned with those around him. Roles are given up, social relationships are restricted in number and scope and there is less commitment to social norms and values." [5]

This theory has been widely discussed by those interested in studying the process of aging. However, not all investigators agree with the theory of disengagement. For instance, Dr. Robert Kastenbaum, Professor of Psychology, Wayne State University, finds that "the disengagement hypothesis assumes that everybody has just about the same kind of

[4] Cummings and Henry, p. 14.   [5] Shanas *et al.*, p. 180.

perspective as they approach the later years of life. This generalization is not tenable," he asserts.[6]

In another study, reported in the *Journal of Gerontology*, the authors came to the conclusion that

> there appears to be substantial evidence for our hypothesis that disengagement among the aged can be predicted to occur as a concomitant of physical or social stress which frequently affects the manner in which the life patterns are redirected. . . . It is not age which produces disengagement, but the impact of physical and social stress which may be expected to increase with aging.[7]

As one considers these different points of view, one is convinced that more study is indicated before a definite conclusion can be reached. Whatever the situation is for some—or all—of the elderly, whether their isolation is the result of society's lack of concern and tendency to exclude them from active participation in community life, or whether there is a tendency on the part of the older person to withdraw, the fact remains that many older people are isolated and lonely, particularly in the small urban communities where transportation facilities are inadequate or totally nonexistent. There is evidence that the problem of transportation for these elderly people, who are frequently homebound, has recently been recognized as important, and it is receiving increased attention.

Availability of Facilities

While the stress of illness, the loss of energy, and the need for dependence are well recognized, there is little appreciation of the social stresses often endured by the elderly,

---

[6] Kastenbaum, p. 131.   [7] Talmer and Kutner, p. 74.

such as the narrowing of the individual's social circle as his contemporaries move away, become ill, or die. It is not easy to make new friends when one is old!

As a result, we find that many of the elderly, divorced from the world of work, feel useless, lonely and isolated and have no way to fill the tedium of long, empty days. This recognition prompted the establishment of facilities to provide social contacts and the opportunity for participation in projects of interest.

The provisions made for a more fruitful utilization of free time have with the passage of years changed in response to the needs and demands of the elderly. The extent to which many of the elderly avail themselves of the opportunity for socialization when it is available to them provides the most forceful refutation of the universal applicability of the theory of disengagement. Not all the elderly wish to disengage themselves, nor do they actually do so. This is evident in the frequency with which they express their dissatisfaction with the segregation to which they are so often consigned, as well as in the eagerness with which they respond to social contacts, meaningful activity, and an opportunity to live a full and productive life. This is true not only of those older individuals whose valuable contributions to society are cited so often, but of older people in all walks of life.

RECREATIONAL FACILITIES

In response to the demands of the elderly and recognizing the importance of their needs, society has developed a variety of day centers under different names, such as Golden Age Clubs, Senior Citizen centers, and others. These centers go far beyond the original "recreation center" with its emphasis on games and other attempts to while away time. They have enlarged the scope of their services and activities to serve ever larger and more discriminating groups of the aged. Now they are making noticeable progress toward becoming multiservice agencies, offering information, referral, and coordinating services in the many areas of need which the elderly encounter. More and more they are being staffed by professional personnel.

Various governmental agencies are beginning to take an interest in these programs and to give financial assistance to make improvements possible. In New York State, for instance, the State Department of Education furnishes state aid on a matching basis, and uses all the resources of adult education for the training of staff and the expansion of significant programs.

The upsurge of interest and activity in meaningful free-time activities for the elderly is evident also among the labor unions. For example, the Amalgamated Clothing Workers of America is cooperating with the New York City Department of Social Services in conducting a center for retired workers in the clothing industry. The program is based on their interest in the union and in developments that affect the labor force. In this way, the retired workers are not completely separated from their work interest, even though they can no longer participate as active members.

This and similar centers meet various needs. They serve to relieve the tedium which often sets in following retirement; they offer worthwhile activities designed to compensate for the lack of participation in the accustomed world of work, and they encourage social contacts to combat the enforced isolation.

Despite the appeal of such centers and the unquestionable service which they render, it must be admitted that they have some undesirable limitations. An important drawback is the fact that the scheduled activities are geared predominantly (and even exclusively) to the needs of the elderly so that they are confined to an association with their own age group. This drawback is being recognized, and an attempt is being made to overcome it by encouraging younger family members to take part in the activities of the center on special occasions. In some instances, programs are being organized to include the young as well as the elderly.

Much has been done to expand the scope and improve the programs of centers for the elderly. Much more remains to be done to insure that their manifold needs are being met.

EDUCATIONAL OPPORTUNITIES

There are in our society many elderly who feel that having worked hard, having raised their children and discharged their duty to society, they now want and have a right to take it easy, sit back, be entertained, and have "a good time."

There are others, interested in continuing intellectual pursuits, for whom existing recreational facilities fail to furnish sufficient stimulation. To serve this group there has been inaugurated under the leadership of Dr. Hyman Hirsh, a new educational institution, the Institute for Retired Professionals of the New School for Social Research in New York City. Dr. Hirsh describes the philosophy of the Institute as follows:

Unfortunately, most programs for the retired are merely stop gaps and provide only diversions, such as arts and crafts, games, sports, and dancing. For the person of some education and skill, stop gaps and diversions are not enough. I say that the answer to retirement leisure for the professional person is challenge.[8]

While one might question the accuracy of Dr. Hirsh's statement about the programs of the centers in the light of

[8] Hirsh, p. 36.

present-day developments, one must agree with his contention that the answer to retirement is "challenge." Dr. Hirsh further points out that a university "with the enrollment of different generations would be one way to close the generation gap, because all generations would meet on the basis of pursuit of learning." [9]

Although Dr. Hirsh has singled out the professionals as the ones who could enrich their retirement years by pursuing such avenues of challenge as are offered by the Institute, it is important to keep in mind that the same program could be of value to many nonprofessionals. Among them are many who have intellectual interests and inner resources who may need the opportunity for further learning and require the stimulation and interaction with others of similar background and comparable interests. Without such stimulation and interaction, their potentialities are in danger of withering and dying.

The contribution made by the Institute program has been recognized as important, and other schools in the country have followed its lead, preserving the general philosophy underlying the approach adopted by the Institute, but making such changes in the curriculum as were needed to meet the requirements of the people they serve.

There is ample evidence to support the belief that many of the elderly are capable of learning and absorbing new knowledge. This was demonstrated by the experience of the schools that have offered an opportunity for continued education. In addition, there is supportive evidence in an experiment conducted by the Institute of Psychological Research at Teachers College, Columbia University. Some 270 individuals between the ages of 45 and 70 were enrolled in a

[9] *Ibid.*, p. 41.

class in Russian, a language to which none of them were previously exposed. Many of the students were apprehensive, feeling that they were "too old to learn." A report of the experiment shows that after two months, these elderly people absorbed the same material as is covered by college students in a semester.

NEED FOR NEW ROLES

Important as are the existing recreational and educational opportunities suited to the needs of some of the elderly, they do not represent the total answer for meeting all the requirements of older people. Many of the elderly are overcome by feelings of uselessness and frustration as they find themselves removed from the surrounding active world. These people, raised in a culture which emphasizes the importance of productivity, miss the satisfaction which they can derive only from a productivity of their own choice and the status which such activity confers. This applies with particular force to those elderly who are vigorous in mind and body, and who find that they have been deprived of such satisfaction by an arbitrarily determined age.

The appreciation of the importance of employing the interests and energy of these people has led within recent years to the development of a number of projects. These undertakings have demonstrated their value both in combatting the feeling of uselessness and in contributing to the welfare of the community. They have shown that the elderly are capable of useful participation in worthwhile endeavors, can attain the sense of independence which they had temporarily lost, and earn the recognition of others in the community. As they themselves express it, "life is again worth living."

Because of the importance which such endeavors have in helping to use the potentials inherent in older people and reclaiming them from the futility and depression to which they often succumb, it may be helpful to discuss some of them in greater detail.

As one example, one might cite the Foster Grandparents' program, first reported in 1966, which now employs some four thousand older men and women who care for double that number of children in need of attention, love, and help. The efforts of the foster grandparents have proved so successful that they have earned the enviable appellation of "child savers."

The success of this program has led to its adoption in other settings. Thus, we find that in 1968 there appeared a report of a program using older people as mental health aides working in cooperation with schools to help children in the lower grades who presented problems in the classroom such as underachievement, withdrawal, or acting out. The older people selected for this program varied in background and education. Before proceeding to work individually with children, they were given a period of orientation and training.

It was found that these older people were "receptive to new learning and quite open in their approach to new ways" of doing things. They were supervised both formally and informally by regular staff members of the mental health clinic services. The results achieved were evaluated independently both by the retirees and the school teachers, and there appeared to be considerable unanimity as to the success of the program, which was manifested in the improvements shown in the children's behavior as well as in their better learning ability.

According to the report, the experiment demonstrated that retired people can be effectively utilized as non-professionals in a professional setting. . . . The experience is an enjoyable and meaningful one for the participants who profited from it. The retirees' favorable reaction to the experiment can be considered as a clue to the reason for the satisfaction they derived from it. The older people felt that the experience gave them the opportunity to apply their wisdom and experience to a worthwhile task. [The study concludes that] there is no reason to assume that schools are the only setting in which retired people can function effectively. . . . The findings suggest that retired people may constitute an important human service resource.[10]

The value of the services of older people in a program designed for service to the elderly was emphasized in a study conducted by the National Council on Aging. The purpose of the project was to involve a large segment of the local older poor in the rural war on poverty. The older people were employed to locate elderly people who needed service; arrange for information and referral; organize groups for self-service; render a variety of personal services to the homebound and, in the process of doing so, involve others in rendering such services.

The report felt that through such participation the elderly are brought out of their isolation. It points out that lack of economic self-sufficiency, poor health, and other disabilities are largely responsible for depriving older people of an opportunity to participate in the life around them. Beginning with the one-to-one relationship, there was at times in the project a spontaneous development of groups in which the elderly themselves perceived areas of need which could be helped through group action. It was found that many of the elderly "can meet the criteria set up for staff selection and

[10] Cowen *et al.*, p. 907.

can participate in programs for children as teachers' aides, as well as cooks, cafeteria aids, drivers, story tellers, carpenters, arts and craft aids, seamstresses, parents' helpers, etc." [11]

The program demonstrated that the elderly can be usefully employed at a variety of tasks, and that they derive satisfaction from helping others rather than having things done for them. In his recognition that he is able to help others, the older person rediscovers a feeling of status, both in his own eyes and in the eyes of others. The implications of this finding, as it affects the older person's position in the family and family relationships are obvious.

Another example of the attempt to utilize the unused potentials of the elderly in serving other elderly who need help is the project SERVE (Serve and Enrich Retirement by Volunteer Experience) of the Community Service Society on Staten Island, New York. Here older volunteers serve in hospitals, schools, and other organizations. The work they perform is diversified and consists of direct person-to-person services as well as helping in the sewing rooms and supply rooms of hospitals. The success of this program has resulted in New York State undertaking similar programs on a statewide basis. The volunteers themselves point out that the major value of their activity lies not so much in what they do for others, but in what it has done for them as people who now have a reason to be alive and who can find satisfaction not known in "old age" before.

Perhaps the greatest satisfaction which the elderly person can derive from pursuing a worthwhile goal comes when he is given an opportunity to continue in his chosen career, or in areas related to it. In a study conducted by Nova University in Florida, a questionnaire was distributed to a

[11] Chandler, *op. cit.*, p. 17.

sample population of some 600 scientists retired from the staffs of certain universities during a certain period. The replies indicated that many of them were "active, interested and retained their zest for living." Many could continue to serve after retirement in a reduced capacity. Most of them were occupied in pursuits related or similar to their career fields. Although the financial return was inadequate without outside supplementation, they enjoyed their work because they could work without pressure. Others were seeking employment; their main reason for doing so was their unfavorable reaction to too much free time and a "desire for continued accomplishment and a need for contact with others of similar interests." [12]

These are but a few illustrations of projects that call upon the abilities of the elderly. There are many others. However, programs which allow for the application of the skills, experience, and wisdom of the elderly have been hampered until recently by a lack of understanding and appreciation of the potentials of the older person. It can only be explained by the general attitude of our society, which is oriented to the present and the future with little regard for the past, as well as by our lack of faith in the elderly. This lack of faith is manifested in the very need to demonstrate to ourselves and to others that the elderly can indeed perform satisfactorily, and by our surprise, at times, when we see older people performing so well on the jobs they undertake.

This attitude is reflected in the small number of elderly people who are employed in the United States, contrasting sharply with the number employed in other countries, such as France and Japan. One might speculate as to the reasons, whether it is due to a difference in attitude toward old age

[12] Gelber, p. 5.

in general, the absence of social security provisions, or the emphasis on industrial advancement, as seen in Japan for example.

The desire of older people to continue working has been amply demonstrated by the program "Mature Temps," established in April, 1969, by the American Association of Retired Persons in response to a growing request by elderly people for temporary employment in order to be kept occupied and to supplement their inadequate income. So successful was the initial trial that efforts are now being made to establish Mature Temps wherever there is a concentration of the Association membership. A typical comment from employers was: "If we could just get the younger workers to work the way the older ones do." It is estimated that "by the end of the third year Mature Temps will be in operation in a hundred cities." [13]

It is hoped that the demonstration of the ability of older people will result in more innovative programs in the future. It seems a sad commentary that we need so many demonstrations of the fact, which we should have known all along, that ability does not cease merely because an individual becomes eligible for social security and that experience, skill, and, most importantly, wisdom are assets too valuable to thrust aside, neglect, and allow to deteriorate. What we need are not gadgets, nor devised ways to "kill time," but an opportunity for the elderly to exercise self-determination and derive satisfaction through creativity and through a contribution to the community.

[13] Mature Temps Birthday Promise," p. 65.

Effect of Extended Free Time on Family Relationships

The excess of free time which is imposed by retirement creates problems not only for the elderly, but for the members of their families as well.

The separation of older persons from their accustomed routine and associations does not affect all of them in the same way. There are those who feel that because they are not working, they are no longer needed or wanted. Some of them, unable to accept their changed status, the loneliness, and the uselessness, tend to become dependent on the younger generation for the satisfaction of their social and emotional needs.

Family members, confronted with the unhappiness of their elders and concerned for their welfare, may attempt to cope with the apathy and discouragement. They may feel that they must somehow provide the companionship and social activities which the elderly are missing—an effort which may prove difficult for them and unsatisfactory for the older person. Rarely does it achieve its objective no matter how good the intent.

It is for this reason that the centers and various projects prove to be such a boon both for the elderly and for their families. The older person, having a place to go and an occupation which interests him, instead of sitting dejectedly at home or tagging along with his children, achieves a revived feeling of independence and importance. At the same time, whatever activities occupy the older person's time have value for the children and their attitude toward the elderly.

As the younger members of the family watch the members of the older generation engage in productive activity and see the respect with which they are regarded by the center staff or their employers, they gain a better understanding of their worth and an appreciation of the contribution of which they are capable.

8. SOCIAL WORK WITH THE ELDERLY

IN ORDER TO DETERMINE the applicability of social work skills and techniques in dealing with the problems of the elderly and with the difficulties these problems often intensify in their relationship with the younger generation, it is essential that we examine the aims and the general philosophy underlying social work practice.

The Aim of Social Work

The aim of social work is to help the individual to attain as full, productive, and meaningful a life as his condition permits, so as to enable him to participate to the fullest extent of his capacities in the life of his family and of the community. It is through such participation that the individual can achieve the satisfaction of belonging and a feeling of worth and status.

This general aim forms the basis of all areas of activity in whatever field and under whatever auspices social work is being practiced. The method employed in rendering the necessary services to achieve this aim may change from time to time as it is influenced and enriched by expanding knowledge and understanding of what may be helpful in any particular situation.

This aim is as valid in dealing with the elderly as it is when working with any other age group. In order to facilitate the application of proven methods and techniques to the problems encountered by the elderly and to the restoration of a satisfactory intergenerational relationship, we need two important ingredients: (1) an appreciation of the variety, the extent, and the severity of the problems the aged encounter; and (2) a conviction that both the older and the younger generations have potentials for change to mitigate the destructive effects of existing difficulties.

Development of the Present-Day Concepts

Social work with the elderly developed in the same way as social work with other age groups, though not at the same time. As we view the developments in the field of social work, we can identify three distinct phases.

Phase I. This period was characterized by a spontaneous, humane response to suffering by rendering such specific help as the provision of food, shelter, and clothing to the poverty-stricken members of the community, the elderly among them. It was assumed that the unhappy condition in which the poor found themselves was due primarily, or even exclusively, to their personal inadequacies. Consequently, no attempt was made—for none seemed to be indicated— to understand the special circumstances which might have been responsible for their plight. As a result, there was little evidence of serious inquiry as to what might be done to eliminate the precipitating causes. Thus, no progress was made toward possible changes.

Phase II. It was not until the beginning of the twentieth century that there was indication of a development in the direction of an increased understanding that mere almsgiving served only as a temporary palliative, alleviating symptoms but failing to eliminate underlying causes. As this understanding developed, we saw the emergence of appreciation that, if meaningful help is to be rendered to the socially deprived, it is necessary not only to meet the end result of social neglect or personal inadequacy in adjusting to the existing conditions, but to foresee—and perhaps forestall—their occurrence. It became recognized that only in this way could the problem of dependence eventually be solved.

This new direction in the approach to poverty demanded of the social work practitioner the acquisition of new knowledge about the multiple causes of dependency, and the development of new techniques in dealing with it. The extended education which this entailed led to what we now know as professional social work.

Social work with the elderly, however, failed to keep pace with this general development. Aging, it was reasoned, was a natural phenomenon, as were the dislocations accompanying it. Since the difficulties encountered by the elderly were part of the process of aging, they were not amenable to outside help or to change. Therefore, there was little that society could do, and it was up to the individual to adjust to his condition.

As late as 1940, we find evidence that the deterioration of the elderly, their isolation, and their progressive inability to deal with their difficulties were considered beyond the scope of social work endeavor. The fact that the other help-

ing professions—particularly the medical profession, to which
social work looked for guidance—showed disinterest in the
welfare of the elderly did little to improve the situation.
Social work continued for a long time to accept the earlier
concept of personal inadequacy as the reason for the deprivations the aging experienced—indeed, long after this approach was abandoned when dealing with younger individuals.

Phase III. As knowledge accumulated, there appeared a
change in emphasis in social work practice. It became recognized that the difficulties with which the social worker was
called upon to deal did not necessarily result from the individual's inability to adjust to existing conditions. Often
they represented an appropriate response to conditions ini-
mical to his welfare. This new understanding involved the
social work practitioner in an attempt to alter unfavorable
conditions and brought about the development of new
techniques necessary for this activity.

At the same time, social work education began to focus
by slow stages not only on a better understanding of social
problems as they are affected by external conditions but,
more significantly, on the need to develop a better comprehen-
sion of the individual's response to the difficulties these conditions create for him. As a result of this training, social workers
became more and more concerned with the persons whom they
were attempting to help, involving a gradual change in their
attitude, a greater sensitivity to inner unexpressed needs, and the
development of empathy coupled with objectivity and flexibility in meeting and responding to the demands made on
them. Social work became "client-centered."

Here again, there was a lag between the enhanced understanding which was manifested in the general field of social

work and the practice so far as the elderly were concerned. It is only recently that the impact of growing numbers of elderly in our society has succeeded in eliciting a minimal response from the social work profession. As experience in working with the elderly accumulated, social work practitioners were brought face to face with the realization that aging is not a thing apart from life, but an integral part of the life cycle which is a continuation from birth to death; that growth and development do not necessarily cease at any predetermined age, and that therefore the aged person often retains the ability to change and can profit by the help extended to him.

With this heightened understanding there came a gradual change in the attitude of the social work profession toward the elderly and an ability to recognize and accept the fact that the elderly, like the rest of us, are people with differing personalities, diverse needs, and dissimilar potentialities for utilizing such help as may be available to them to achieve a more satisfactory adjustment.

Despite this developed understanding, it is important to recognize that interest in social services to the aged is even now limited to a certain extent, and is being considered, in many instances, as barely deserving the attention of the professional social worker. The social problems of the aged are still accepted as being inherent in the very process of aging as well as in the older person's inability to make the necessary adjustment to existing conditions.

With the growing number of elderly in our society and the greater complexity of life, the problems of the older person are multiplying. Social work must assume the responsibility for mitigating, wherever possible, the harsh conditions so frequently created by an inflexible society. This service, which has long been the hallmark of social work endeavor, must be made available to the elderly in order to enable them to achieve the aim of social work, formulated earlier, namely, the attainment of a meaningful, satisfying, and productive old age within the limits of their physical and mental capacities.

We are just beginning to see the emerging recognition that the excessive hardships of aging present a challenge for social work concern. Those who devote time and effort, which working with the elderly demands, are learning that the expectation that the older person can adjust to the intolerable conditions of segregation and neglect is both unreasonable and unrealistic. The application of the basic principles of social work and an attempt to change some of the environment in which the elderly live can prove of inestimable value in improving their lot.

Not long ago, the Community Service Society of New York City announced a change in its policy, which recognizes that the problems of the individual often stem from the unfavorable conditions of the community in which he lives. Dr. James G. Emerson Jr., General Director, states:

If the individual is to be helped, someone has to deal with the complex of social ills that bears on the individual, not just on the individual himself. We are convinced that an approach that focuses primarily on individuals may help some people, but will not really alleviate the basic problem of a sick community.[1]

The Society therefore took the "radical step" of declaring that it will henceforth consider the community rather than the individual as its client. While agreeing with the point of view that the problems of the individual are often a response to the unwholesome environment in which he finds himself,

[1] "Community Service Society Dropping Casework to Give Aid to Slum Groups," p. 46.

one cannot help but wonder whether such an exclusive emphasis represents a valid solution to all the problems of distress which are encountered so often.

Areas of Social Work Concern

It would be futile to attempt to enumerate the various ways in which the social work profession can make its services available and acceptable to the elderly. Our previous discussion clearly indicates that the areas where social work is needed are numerous and extend in many directions since aging brings with it a variety of distressful situations: loss or substantial reduction of income; the need for change in living quarters—often a traumatic experience; general increase in physical and mental incapacities; loss of close and significant persons through physical separation and death; estrangement from relatives and friends accentuated by loss of mobility, loss of self-direction, status, role, and purpose in life.

All of these losses often occur simultaneously and in a variety of combinations, bringing with them insecurity and the fear of dependency in the economic, physical, social, or emotional sense. This fear is manifested all too clearly as one listens to the oft-encountered assertion of the older person that he does not wish to grow old if he will not be able to meet his everyday requirements, have the ability to remain independent, and be in reasonably good health.

The Nature of Social Work Services

To provide adequately for the needs of the elderly, social service activities must take into consideration both the elderly person himself and those closely associated with him, mainly the members of his immediate family. The social worker frequently finds that in working both with the older person and with members of his family, she can use successfully the techniques which she employs with other age groups. She finds that she must begin with a study of the situation in order to discover the kind of help the older person requires and to utilize those resources available within herself as well as the facilities in the community which are most suitable to the particular individual.

In addition to helping the elderly person with his problems, as well as helping family members with the difficulties which responsibility for an aging relative entails, the social worker must also become involved in what has been referred to as the "advocacy role." This indicates involvement in those situations where the individual is unable to plan for himself and has no close relative who can plan for him. It may require drastic changes in agency policy and procedures, in community organization, or in the need for wide-scale governmental intervention. The helpfulness of the worker's contribution is determined to a large extent by her ability to share her findings and document them through her first-hand knowledge and experience.

Special Areas of Needed Help

Let us consider in some detail those problems of the elderly which are not often encountered by the social worker in her work with other age groups.

In pursuing the goal of helping the elderly person achieve as satisfying and fulfilling life as his condition allows, the social worker must begin with the older person's capacity for independence and self-direction which characterized him before he reached old age. In addition, she must understand what he expects of himself at this particular stage of his life, the goals to which he aspires, as well as what goals can realistically be projected for the future.

We have emphasized that the techniques which the social worker employs in a helping capacity while dealing with younger people can be utilized successfully in working with the elderly. At the same time, however, the social worker discovers that rendering services to this particular group at times requires a change in the traditional way of functioning, and often necessitates the need to change her concept as to what a social worker does or does not do.

PROBLEMS UNDERLYING REQUEST FOR HELP

Experience has demonstrated that the older person seldom makes a personal application for help. Furthermore, whether the application is made by him or by those concerned with his welfare, it often does not represent what he needs or wants.

Frequently, the initial referral comes to the social agency because the older individual is unable to provide for himself out of his meager resources—a not uncommon situation in view of the general level of income among many of the elderly. There was a time when social workers were inclined to believe that this problem could be simply solved through the granting of adequate relief. A better understanding of the implications of the request brings the realization that the economic problem is not an isolated phenomenon. In this, as in other situations, the request for help and the acceptance of financial assistance are closely related to the individual's feeling of becoming dependent, which is often a complicating factor in his social adjustment.

Going even further, it may bring to the fore rifts in family relationships, resentment about what he considers to be his children's indifference to his plight, and, at the same time, his feelings—whether positive or negative—about receiving financial help from strangers rather than from members of his family. The understanding, or lack of it, of the more deeply seated problems related to the application for financial assistance will determine the kind of service that will be most helpful in this situation.

Similarly, it has been found that an elderly person who applies to a hospital for medical service is likely to concentrate on the symptoms of his physical discomfort because his understanding of the role of a medical institution is that it is to render such help. An attempt by the social worker to delve further into the situation will soon unearth the fact that in addition to the diagnosis established by the physician, there may be a plethora of other problems with which he needs help. Financial difficulties or poor family relationships may be at the root of his physical symptoms. The man's presenting condition may be closely related to poverty, which may have prevented his taking care of his ailments before a critical stage brought him to the doctor. At times, it may prevent his following the doctor's orders if these involve an outlay of money. As an illustration, we can all recall instances where the physican advises a change of climate without inquiring into the patient's ability to meet the cost such a change would involve.

In some instances, the vague aches and pains of which the elderly complain so frequently may mask a feeling of re-

jection and loneliness. The patient may be reluctant to admit these feelings and, since illness does not carry with it
any stigma such as emotional dependence often does, the
older person's complaints may be used to secure the interest
and care he so badly needs. The mere opportunity to talk
to someone who is willing to listen is often used to mitigate
to some extent the feeling of having been abandoned. The
social worker, who is aware of the older patient's difficulties
in this area, can help both by sympathetic listening and by
interpreting the person's underlying feeling to the physician,
thus assuring a more realistic and sympathetic response on
his part.

Another situation in which the services of the social worker
can be of great help to the aged arises when he is faced with
the need to change his living quarters. The fact that the
elderly person expresses a wish for such a change does not
necessarily mean that he is ready to take the necessary steps
toward carrying it out. Nor does it always mean that he
needs to make the change. The social worker who is aware
of the possible meaning of the request can help by ascer-
taining both the actual need for such a move, the person's
actual desire for it, and whatever misgivings he might have.

On the basis of her experience, the social worker is prepared to meet both the hesitancy and the uncertainty, and
to make allowances for the fact that even when a plan is
cheerfully entered into, the older person may change his
mind and decide to abandon it. The extent to which the
social worker is able to accept these reactions and go along
with such changes in needs and desires on the part of the
older person has considerable importance for him. It con-
vinces him that the worker understands him and is really

willing to help him achieve what he desires for himself. On her part, the social worker thus asserts her belief in the older person's ability to think and act in his own best interests; by doing so, she helps the elderly to regain feelings of worth, status, and ability.

MEETING CRISIS SITUATIONS

The older person's resistance to acknowledging the need for outside help, as being indicative of his inability to cope with his situation unaided, means that often his need comes to the attention of the social agency at a point of crisis. While crises occur in the lives of people of all ages, its occurrence in the case of the elderly acquires a sense of particular urgency—the old have no time to wait. Such was the case when Mrs. Blank applied for help (Chapter 7). Her recital of the danger in which her mother found herself when left alone in the house gave evidence of panic. In such instances, the availability of immediate contact with a social worker and the latter's response to the feeling of urgency with a calm discussion of the various ways in which the situation could be met, helped to allay the fear and to find an acceptable solution.

There are also instances when a problem is presented as one of extreme urgency. It may be related to the older person's feeling that for him time is indeed running out, or it may be a means of testing the worker's interest and her understanding of his concern. Under these circumstances, the worker's positive response to what may appear to be unreasonable pressure for prompt action helps to convince the older person that he can turn to her in the future should he be confronted with what he considers to be an emergency. Such a response to a request for immediate action is often different from the deliberate study of a situation, which is the worker's method of procedure in other instances, and it requires a different orientation as to her function.

IMPORTANCE OF A SUPPORTIVE ROLE

Throughout her contact with the older person and regardless of the type of service required and given, the greatest service the social worker can render is in helping him to overcome the feelings of worthlessness and depression which often assail the elderly by emphasizing, whenever opportunity presents itself, the positive values of his greater understanding of life, his experience, and his wisdom—aspects which those around him tend to ignore, deny, or denigrate. The older person, given this kind of support, repeatedly re-emphasized, can be helped to withstand the onslaught of his various incapacities, build up his self-esteem, accept more easily his change in status, and see himself as being a worthwhile person despite his incapacities.

Frequently, in dealing with the elderly, the social worker must adjust to a change in her role as compared to what she considers her role to be in other situations. While there are those elderly who are strong, able to decide on a course of action once the facts are known to them and to proceed in carrying out a plan, there are others who, being old and feeble and having no one to help them, may require assistance with the physical details that a plan may require. These tangible services are new and unfamiliar to the social worker, who, in her dealings with younger people, expects them to assume responsibility for the actual work involved in carrying out a plan. In dealing with the elderly, however, the social worker must accept the necessity of rendering tangible services as part of her total responsibility. At the same time, she must learn to recognize their value to the elderly, who may see them as an indication of her interest and concern.

The need for a mature individual to ask for help brings him face to face with his inadequacy—a feeling difficult for any person to accept, and doubly difficult for the older person who has spent a lifetime building up his concept of self-sufficiency. It not only threatens the individual's self-image, but, in addition, he is fearful that he will lose his role and status with his family members.

While the older person might have needed help in his younger years at times when he was sick or disabled, he could accept it then, knowing that it was temporary and that he would return to his former self as soon as his health improved. The situation is different for the old, who cannot help but be aware that dependency may become for them a way of life. This need to accept dependency as possibly a permanent state often makes them fearful and hostile.

The social worker, if she is to be of help, can neither deny nor encourage expressions of dependency. Instead, she must emphasize existing strengths in encouraging the older person to deal, in so far as he is able, with his problems, while offering such help as he may require to insure that he will not fail. This emphasis on the positive aspects of the older person conveys to him the feeling of respect which the worker has for him and thus helps him to regain some measure of self-respect, and makes it unnecessary for him to emphasize his weakness as a means of achieving recognition and care.

To illustrate the importance of this supportive attitude on the part of the worker, we might consider her role as a medical social worker dealing with patients suffering from prolonged illness, for the problems which confront these patients are not unlike the problems which the elderly must face.

How does the worker help the patient when his condition persists without visible improvement for long periods of time? Such help must be based on the patient's realistic acceptance of his disability, recognizing his limitations and setting new goals for himself on a level appropriate to his condition without attempting to compete in areas which are beyond his ability. It is self-evident that in order to derive satisfaction from newly set goals, these goals must be set in line with his remaining abilities and must be realizable in the not too distant future. This approach can be successfully applied to the elderly as well as to the sick person, and in this way the destructive feelings of inadequacy and frustration, so often encountered, can be minimized.

In attempting to carry out such a plan for restoring a feeling of adequacy, the worker must be able to hear with what has been called "the third ear." In other words, she must listen not only to what is being said, but also to what is being implied and what is not being articulated. This involves, among other things, the ability to accept negative feelings and negative reactions, even when these are directed to the worker herself. It means recognizing and accepting the older person's concern as to what the future might bring, including his fear of death and of being deserted by his family.

Nor is the worker's activity limited to the passive acceptance of what the elderly person brings to her. Recognizing the destructive influences of fears and misgivings, the worker must attempt to direct the person's thoughts and energies as a means of counteracting anxiety, and to involve him in both immediate and future planning. How important such an approach can be, was well formulated by an older man who said: "It restored my self-respect, relieved my fear of being alone and helpless; it restored my faith in humanity."

As in all other social work situations, the opportunity to discuss and share enables the person to become more independent and self-directing.

SERVICES TO FAMILY MEMBERS

The older person is not necessarily alone in facing the difficulties and deprivations which frequently accompany the process of aging. Despite the emphasis on the "generation gap" so prevalent today, strong family ties often bind the two generations. Family members also suffer as they watch the suffering of their elderly relative, and they often require help in coping with their own reactions to his suffering and helplessness. They may need help in making a satisfactory plan for his care, or they may need information about available resources, or they may require encouragement and support in carrying out a plan already made and relief from the feeling of guilt which it frequently provokes.

Thus, help to family members becomes important for the preservation of their own mental health as well as for insuring a better climate for the older person. In helping family members with the various problems that the older relative's adjustment creates, the social worker at the same time improves the relationship existing within the family group.

The following case is an illustration of a situation where the interest of family members was important to the older person and where they had to be involved in planning:

Mrs. Roberts, an 80-year-old widow, lived alone in a furnished room and was able to manage financially on the social security benefits she received.

As age advanced, it became more and more difficult for her to care for her personal needs. Mrs. Roberts felt that "old age is terrible; you are sick; you have to skimp to get along, but you do not want to accept charity; you are alone and nobody cares."

It was evident that something had to be done, but Mrs. Roberts could not say what she wanted.

The worker took her clue from Mrs. Roberts's statement that she was "alone and nobody cares." Realizing that this feeling of being abandoned was uppermost in Mrs. Roberts's mind, she succeeded in having Mrs. Roberts tell her about her family. She learned that Mrs. Roberts had lived with her married daughter at one time, but because of "in-law trouble" she was asked to leave. As she spoke about having been "part of her daughter's family," it was apparent how hurt she was by the rejection.

Since Mrs. Roberts's primary concern was about being alone, it became apparent that her daughter needed to be closely involved in planning and helping her mother. In the process of trying to help Mrs. Roberts, it became necessary to help the daughter with her own problems, namely, the difficulties she had with her husband where Mrs. Roberts was concerned. She needed support to help her discuss the matter with her husband and make him realize her mother's difficulty as well as her responsibility to, and her concern about, her mother and her need to do something about it.

This and many other instances of work with the elderly amply demonstrate the importance of evaluating carefully not only the need for such concrete services as financial assistance, proper medical care, or advice on the advantages or disadvantages of institutional placement, but the value of personal relationships so important to the elderly.

Working with the relatives, helping them as well as the

older person himself, can resolve such problems as may stand in the way of achieving a comfortable and helpful family relationship. Frequently the problems which relatives bring to the social worker are not actually the problems with which they need help. Often at the root of these problems are the anxiety which the incapacity of the older person provokes and the guilt at their inability to cope with it. This was the case with Mrs. Hane:

Mrs. Hane applied to a social agency to secure the help of a homemaker. She explained that her husband had a series of small strokes, which made him dependent on his wife.

This dependence proved difficult for Mrs. Hane to accept. She explained that her husband had been a strong and successful man, and his present helplessness was difficult to bear. She spoke of Mr. Hane as a good husband who always took care of her and protected her from any unpleasantness. Now, he was irritable and difficult to please. Mrs. Hane was disturbed by the change in his personality.

It was evident that Mrs. Hane needed the help of a housekeeper, and this was provided. There were, however, other areas where help seemed to be indicated. Through discussion, and as Mrs. Hane developed confidence in the worker, she was able to see that the picture of Mr. Hane as the perfect husband was not quite accurate. She began to admit that his irritability, although undoubtedly aggravated by his illness, was always there, and that he was always demanding, controlling, and interfering.

Once Mrs. Hane was able to admit it, it became easier for her to accept his present behavior. The guilt which she felt in not being able to care for her husband, and not being "as good a wife as he was a husband," was relieved as she saw the reality of the previously existing marital situation.

Despite our recognition of the importance of contact with relatives and their importance in the care of the older person, actual experience demonstrates that all too often contact with relatives is limited to the application process, and in only a few instances is it extended to continued work with family members. This neglect is frequently explained on the basis that relatives "do not wish to be involved" beyond the point where the pressing problem is appropriately solved.

One can legitimately question whether the problem confronting the elderly is actually solved by taking care of what the relatives present at the time of application. Nor can one assume that the tendency of family members to remove themselves from further planning and treatment is due to their resistance to involvement. Careful examination often indicates that sufficient effort is not always made to involve them, when they do not involve themselves as a matter of course. Is this lack of effort due to the fact that we, as social workers, are too ready to accept the existence of a "generation gap" as unavoidable and proceed to leave the relatives out of further involvement?

If we are ready to help with such negative feelings as may exist, and to strengthen existing positive feelings on the part of family members, we may find that services rendered to family members, who are often burdened with a variety of difficult problems, is a *must* in the process of safeguarding and enhancing the older person's welfare.

The social worker who is aware of the values inherent in family cohesiveness can devise various means to strengthen family relationships. When this is done, family members can be an important help in meeting difficulties in all the areas of the older person's needs.

To utilize her skills effectively toward this end, the difficulties which the older person's condition creates for the family must be understood, and adequate help must be provided. The family must be given an understanding of the older person's condition, his needs, and his feelings; they must be involved in planning when the older person's condition worsens, thus helping the elderly remain part of the family circle—a circle in which he had played such an important part in the past. Old age, even with all its attending incapacities, must not be allowed to remove him from the interest and concern of his family. On the contrary, it is at this time of life that he most needs the warmth, support, and understanding of those close to him, if he is to be helped to adjust to the crises and losses of aging.

Continued contact with family members is important, not only in the help they can give in the care of their relative, but, equally important, it can help them to handle their own problems as they attempt to cope with the physical strain and emotional tension which the witnessing of the older person's difficulties creates for them.

How helpful such services can be, is illustrated in the case of Mr. and Mrs. Borden (Chapter 7). It would have been easy for the social worker to withdraw from the situation at the point when the children undertook to meet the parents' deficit and arrived at an equitable distribution of responsibility. However, the worker was aware of the sibling rivalry and the parents' favoritism and was sensitive to the possibility of friction which would affect adversely the welfare of the old folks. She therefore remained in close contact with all three children, in person, when possible, as well as by correspondence, keeping all three informed of what was happening to the parents and calling upon them for the help they could give as changes occurred in their parents' situation.

How important this help was, is expressed in the letter one of the sons wrote to the worker at the end of the contact. It said in part:

During the time of our contact, I never thanked you for the assistance you have given my parents during the difficult days of the past year. I want you to know how comforted we were not only by the help you have given them, but also by your understanding of our position, your perception of our need for your help. I am confident that my brother and sister share my gratitude.

SOCIAL WORK AND INSTITUTIONAL CARE

We have discussed the children's difficulties in understanding and accepting institutional care for their parent, as well as the difficulties which the older person himself faces in accepting such care. The understanding of these difficulties imposes on the social worker the responsibility of helping the older person accept the necessary care as well as helping him in his adjustment to institutional living. The milieu in which he finds himself is different from anything he has experienced earlier, it presents some frightening aspects, and his satisfactory adjustment to it has an important bearing on his welfare.

The worker's role in this situation is not confined to the one-to-one relationship with the elderly person. If she is to be helpful to him, she must establish a relationship with the institutional staff and contribute her knowledge and understanding of the person's needs, desires, his ability (or lack of it) to adjust to unfamiliar surroundings, reactions—both positive and negative—which can be anticipated, and the help he will need in this process of adjustment.

Because of the importance of the staff's attitude to the resident, it is essential to convey to them an understanding of the meaning of their relationship to him. The social worker knows that the elderly person may carry over to the institutional staff some of the feelings and reactions which characterized his relationship with members of his family. This may be an asset in some instances, but decidedly injurious in others. Members of the institutional staff, who are often untrained, however, frequently tend to perpetuate such a relationship without an understanding of, or regard for, its positive or negative value. If the social worker is successful in interpreting the resident's behavior and the staff's response to it, the staff can be helped to adjust their reaction and response in a more productive manner.

Nor can the worker be content with merely helping in the older person's initial adjustment to the institution. She must be prepared to maintain contact for a prolonged period of time. It can be helpful to the elderly person in assuring him of the continued interest of the person whom he had learned to trust, of having a sympathetic listener, as well as someone with whom he can discuss the minor irritations which can often arise and with which she is able to help him. Even when the elderly person has continued contact with his family, there are many instances where the continued interest of the social worker has values which family members are unable to provide.

ADVOCACY ROLE OF THE SOCIAL WORKER

We take it for granted that it is the responsibility of responsible citizenship to help eliminate such inequities as exist in our society and to improve conditions in the community by instituting whatever measures may be necessary to insure a more satisfying life for all its citizens. The social worker shares this responsibility of citizenship. Furthermore, her newly awakened appreciation of the fact that unacceptable conditions are often responsible for the lack of adjustment of the people whom she is trying to help, imposes on her an added obligation to assume a role in activities designed to ameliorate existing conditions. Her contribution can have particular significance because of her firsthand knowledge of the needs of the people whom she serves as well as of the inadequate facilities available to meet these needs. If this knowledge and experience are to be effective, it is important that they be shared with those leaders in the community who help to determine the policies governing the activities of the private philanthropic organizations, and with the legislators who determine the provisions of assistance granted under governmental auspices.

Traditionally, private philanthropic organizations assumed the role of demonstrating existing needs and ways of meeting them. This was the case in helping to initiate governmental action in the field of income maintenance which resulted in public assistance, as well as in Medicare and Medicaid, and in inaugurating a program of housing suitable to the needs of older people.

As an illustration of the contribution which the individual social worker can make, let us consider the case of Mr. Jordan:

> Mr. Jordan, a 75-year-old man with no surviving relatives, lived alone in a small apartment, where he maintained himself successfully. All went well until he fell, injuring his leg, which made it impossible for him to continue caring for himself.
>
> He was admitted to a hospital where it was discovered that, in addition to his leg injury, Mr. Jordan suffered from a number of other ailments and was in a generally debili-

tated condition, apparently due to his poor eating habits.

When Mr. Jordan was ready to leave the hospital, it was felt that he was not in a condition to care for himself. Since he insisted on returning to his apartment and refused to consider any other arrangement, efforts were made to secure some part-time housekeeping service.

There were numerous social agencies in the community, and the social worker got in touch with all of them in an effort to secure either a housekeeper or a home aide. It was also necessary to arrange for someone to transport Mr. Jordan to the doctor's office for follow-up treatment.

It was found, however, that despite the plethora of agencies, it was impossible to secure the service required by Mr. Jordan. In some, the waiting list for the service was long; others did not have enough housekeepers. Home aides could be supplied only on a one-day-a-week basis. Nursing services were not available for people suffering from chronic conditions. Still other agencies were restricted by their rigid definition of their function.

Since Mr. Jordan could not remain in his apartment alone, the worker finally succeeded in persuading him to consider a nursing home. She was able to locate eight nursing homes in the community. Most of them were rejected because of their deplorable condition; others had rigid admission policies which made Mr. Jordan ineligible. At one home operated by the local welfare organization, Mr. Jordan was rejected, although the worker could not obtain a clear statement as to the reason for the rejection.

In all, the worker established contact with seventeen organizations without securing the care which Mr. Jordan needed.

Disturbed by the absence of suitable facilities to care for Mr. Jordan and others like him, the worker submitted a detailed report of her unsuccessful efforts to the director of the agency which employed her. This had two favorable effects. The director, having been given proof of the need in the community, called a meeting of all the agencies concerned. The interest thus aroused, resulted in an application to the Administration on Aging and the eventual establishment of an office on aging to coordinate all facilities for better service to the aged in the community. Moreover, appalled by Mr. Jordan's plight, the agency solicited private contributions to pay for his stay in a nursing home, whose rates were higher than the agency could afford to pay, until he was sufficiently recovered to return to his apartment.

To her work with Mr. Jordan, the worker not only brought her professional skill as a helping person, but initiated steps to modify unfavorable social conditions. While this situation presents an extreme picture of the rigidities and inadequacies of the service organizations in one community, the situation described occurs in many other localities. The social worker's concern for the welfare of one particular elderly person was helpful in instituting much needed community organization changes.

Unfortunately, such participation in social action is not always characteristic of the profession of social work. Social workers, as a rule, lack the aggression or the know-how necessary to achieve the cooperation of administrative personnel or political leaders. It is only recently that we can detect steps in that direction. While we may deplore the lack of participation in the broader social issues, which characterized the profession until recent times, we must take into consideration the early beginnings of social work with its emphasis on dispensing charity rather than on attempting to better social conditions. It takes time for attitudes to change as well as a willingness to accept the need for change.

Qualities Required in Work with the Elderly

Work with the elderly and the need to deal with their very difficult problems require the same skills and techniques as those which apply in any casework situation and which are absorbed by the worker during her training and through the experience in working with other age groups.

As in any other casework situation, the exercise of these skills and techniques would fail to achieve the desired results if in applying them, the worker were unable to convey her genuine interest, understanding, concern, warmth, and sensitivity. The elderly, so often deprived in these areas, are especially responsive to any evidence of understanding. In addition, it is extremely important that the older person's frailty should not jeopardize the worker's acceptance of his potentials, that she safeguard his right to make decisions affecting his future, and remember at all times that the elderly are particularly vulnerable in their need for understanding and acceptance because of their age and status.

As an example we might cite the skill and sensitivity with which the social worker enabled Mrs. Blau (Chapter 4) to face the reality of her advanced age and limitations—both of which Mrs. Blau denied to herself as well as to others— without attacking her defenses and without arousing any guilt or embarrassment. Similarly, other cases (Mrs. Black Chapter 5; Mrs. Hane *supra*) illustrate the worker's ability to recognize that what is originally requested may not necessarily be the best solution to the problem, but is sometimes being suggested in order to ask for help indirectly. Recognizing this, the worker is able to respond to the underlying but not verbalized request.

The struggle between the need to be dependent and the feeling that they should be independent, which the elderly often experience, presents a special problem for the social worker. The latter, reared in a culture which regards dependency as a lack of maturity, may find herself unable to tolerate dependency in an older person. This reaction is further aggravated by the worker's youth and her own efforts to free herself of her remaining dependent attitudes; it requires a very mature person indeed to be able to accept the fact that dependent attitudes persist in most of us, including the old. Whether greater independence is ever achieved or not depends on a variety of factors in the life of the individual as well as on the particular stresses of the moment. In arriving at such an understanding, the social worker may discover that enabling the older person to accept some measure of dependency without undue struggle may be a worthwhile accomplishment.

The worker must also be able to recognize that dependency can be used to serve the needs of the individual in any particular instance. Sometimes, the actual limitations imposed by illness or incapacity are in themselves insufficient to account for the individual's feeling of utter inadequacy and his tendency to lean on the worker. Such dependency may be due not only to the actual limitation, but to the individual's emotional reaction to it which interferes with his ability to utilize sufficiently his remaining potentials. If the worker is to be helpful, it is essential that she be able to see the person unobscured by his disability. She must also have a knowledge of the way he functioned in the past and the extent to which he required outside help and support in reaching the goals which he set for himself.

Such knowledge and understanding can best be attained

through an interest in, and careful listening to, the older
person as he tries to communicate through his reminiscences.
Such recitals of his past are used by the older person to convey to the worker a picture of himself as an adequate individual who met his responsibilities to his family and to the
community and received recognition for his efforts. In this
way, the older person impresses upon the worker the fact
that he was not always the person she now knows. It requires
considerable experience to determine the accuracy of the
picture of adequacy and complete independence.

The recital of past accomplishments also provides the
worker with a better understanding than she could otherwise
obtain as to what the individual has set for himself as a life
goal, whether or not this goal was ever reached, and a clearer
appreciation of the frustrations which his disability imposes
on him. At the same time, it helps her in determining what
goals would be satisfactory to the older individual at this
time of his life. While it is true that the goals of the person
in his youth and his maturity may not be applicable when
he is old and perhaps incapacitated, nevertheless they can
help to indicate what can be aspired to and expected to provide suitable gratification in the present.

This ability to listen attentively to what may appear to
others to be merely repetitious ramblings has an additional
value for the worker's relationship with the older person.
The interest which she manifests can make the elderly feel
that his past life, which has such meaning to him, has also
a meaning to someone else. At the same time, the discussion
which centers on setting goals for the future can help to
eliminate the feeling of uselessness and the fear of having
lost all personal worth, while offering something of value
to look forward to.

Recent Trends in Social Work

Growing recognition of the numerous problems which beset ever increasing numbers of older people led to a greater appreciation of the necessity of providing essential casework services to help cope with these needs. This, in turn, has led to far-reaching developments in the field of social work. Among these are: (1) emerging evidence of considerably more awareness on the part of social work schools, of the need to acquaint their students with the problems of the older generation; (2) a more extensive utilization of non-professional personnel in social work agencies to provide the necessary services; and (3) the use of group work techniques to supplement the one-to-one relationship, previously used exclusively in social casework, as a means of helping selected groups of aged to cope with their problems.

INTEREST OF SCHOOLS OF SOCIAL WORK

Interest of the schools of social work and recogntion of the need to prepare workers for this particular field of endeavor followed the growth of interest in the aged on the part of the community as a whole.

Until comparatively recently, emphasis in these schools centered primarily, or even exclusively, on training workers to understand and deal with problems of children, young adults, and mature individuals involved in difficult marital problems. No courses designed specifically to acquaint social work students with the problems of the elderly were listed in the curricula. It was only when members of a family with which students were working during their course

of training were confronted with the problems of their elderly relatives, that they received consideration. Even then,
the emphasis in most instances was not so much on the difficulties confronting the older person himself, but mostly
on the way in which these difficulties affected the younger
members of the family group.

This attitude on the part of schools of social work reflected the attitude of social agencies until the late 1930s and
early 1940s. The schools as well as the agencies resisted involvement in services to the aged of the community. Within recent years, the heightened interest in the field of aging
and in the services that older people require is reflected in
an increased interest on the part of some of the schools.
There is now a realization that the elderly have many problems, some of which are identical with the problems of
younger age groups; others are created by the process of
aging, or are inflicted on the elderly by the rejecting attitude
of the society in which they live, and by the lack of facilities
available for their care.

The amount of attention given to the aged as a special
group requiring specialized services is still minimal. Nevertheless, some of the schools include a discussion of the problems of the aged in the general course on human growth and
development, thus giving recognition to the fact that aging
is part of the life cycle, and that the elderly are capable of
growing and developing despite their advanced age. Other
schools include discussions of the problems of the elderly
in courses devoted to study, diagnosis, and treatment. There
is also emphasis on the need to understand the individual
older person a well as the interaction between him and the
younger members of his family. Courses are being introduced dealing with the psychosocial aspects of aging with

emphasis on such changes as occur with isolation, with depletion of resources, with the loss of a significant role in life; the social and emotional effects of retirement; the reaction to illness and to the approach of disability and death. The Columbia University School of Social Work, for instance, gives a course on biopsychosocial aspects of aging. Other schools, such as the one at Syracuse University, New York, have done a great deal to promote student interest in the aging and their problems in the hope of arousing interest in working with this particular group.

Students are being placed for training in agencies dealing with the problems of the elderly, as well as in hospitals caring for long-term patients, the majority of whom are often elderly. The Columbia University School of Social Work uses day centers for group work training; the Adelphi University School of Social Work in Garden City, New York, has assigned graduate students to several New York State projects. Experience has demonstrated the importance of placing students in agencies where standards are high and where the general atmosphere is one of interest and concern with the welfare of the elderly. When placed in agencies with low standards or a lack of demonstrable interest in work, the students become discouraged by the unavailability of facilities needed to provide the help the elderly require and react with a feeling of hopelessness in attempting to provide for such needs. As a result, they may choose some other field of social work upon graduation.

While there is evidence of attempts on the part of some schools to arouse the interest of the students in this particular field of social work, members of the school faculties, with notable exceptions, are still reluctant to become involved in this field. In some instances, there is a lack of training facilities for the teaching and supervision of students, and this seems to discourage the teaching staff. In one instance, a faculty adviser expressed her feeling that it was not her role to focus on the aging as an area of possible interest, though she would tell students about it, if asked. In extreme cases, students who expressed interest in this field were discouraged by advisers who emphasized the fact that there is "no future in it."

CHOICE OF PERSONNEL

The other factor which is often responsible for the lack of desire on the part of social workers to enter this particular field is that too little attention is being given to the kind of person most suitable for it.

The young social worker may have had little professional experience with aging, sickness, or death. She finds, when she is exposed to them, difficulty in dealing with the often tragic aspects of the older person's life, and is therefore hesitant to confine her professional interest to this particular group. It has been found that, in working with the elderly, the social worker is confronted with the need to develop attitudes which are difficult for young people. She may be expected to help with emotional problems between the older person and his children which closely parallel those she is experiencing in her relation to her parents and grandparents. For instance, even if she has no direct experience, she may react to the fact that dealing with her grandparents' difficulties consumes too much time and attention on the part of one or another of her parents. Thus, whether she has been exposed to some of the problems afflicting the elderly in her own family group, or has not been exposed at all, it may be difficult for her to develop the empathy and objectivity which this work requires.

On the other hand, the older person entering this field of social work may be approaching the age at which the various difficulties she encounters in working with the aged may at times force her to realize that she herself may soon have to face similar problems. The heavy burden this is likely to impose on her may not only be difficult to bear, but may even make it impossible to attain the necessary objectivity and to avoid too strong an identification with the people she is attempting to help.

It would seem, then, that the only choice left to those engaged in recruiting workers for this area of social work would be among the not-so-young and the not-so-old, students in the middle-age group who are mature enough to handle the emotionally charged problems which occur so often among the elderly. The attainment of this objective presents serious realistic difficulties. Nor is such conclusion necessarily valid. New workers bring to any situation memories and attitudes from the past, old ways of doing things, ingrained hopes, fears, and beliefs, some of which may contribute to, while others may detract from, their ability to perform satisfactorily. Thus, both the older and the younger workers could profit from help with whatever problems stand in the way of their functioning. Experience shows that such difficulties as present themselves can be resolved.

Fortunately, there are signs of changing attitudes among the school faculties and among the students' advisers and supervisors. The growing emphasis which is being given to the problems of the elderly in some schools is an important beginning and indicates that more can and will be done in the future. The very pressure of the older people's needs will insure greater attention. So far, however, social work with the elderly is still not being given the recognition and importance it deserves. Priorities are still not being assigned to this important problem in most, if not all, schools of social work.

USE OF PROFESSIONALLY UNTRAINED PERSONNEL

Despite the increasing numbers of social workers being graduated by schools of social work, there is a widening gap between the need for essential services in all fields of social work and the availability of professionally trained personnel to meet this need. As a result, some agencies have turned to nonprofessionally trained personnel. This so-called "solution" to the problem has been accepted in various areas of social work endeavor and is widespread among agencies dealing with the elderly.

As a justification of this practice, agencies point to the inescapable truth that there are just not enough professionally trained workers. At the same time, many services can be effectively rendered by nonprofessionally trained people under proper supervision—services which do not need to occupy the time of a highly trained staff. At the same time, the professional staff is in some instances not only willing but eager to assign these time-consuming matters to nonprofessional aides.

There is, however, a great deal of difference between assigning an aide to relieve social workers of the many details which the care of the elderly often involves, and assigning a total caseload to a nonprofessional worker to handle in all its aspects, including such emotional problems as care of the aged frequently involves, with the idea that these can be adequately handled because there is professional supervision. For instance, it is one thing to have an aide locate a suitable apartment for an elderly person, take him to inspect it, or even help him with the physical task of moving. It is quite another to have the aide discuss with the older person his reactions to the need for such a step. There is a world of difference between having the aide accompany the elderly person to a clinic after the doctor and the social worker have thoroughly discussed with him the necessity for such care, as against assigning to the aide the responsibility for discussing these plans with the individual concerned.

On the other hand, aides could be fruitfully utilized to visit long-term cases who do not require or cannot use casework services, and where the visits are designed to maintain contact with an isolated individual through a representative of the agency. It would be necessary, however, for the aide to leave the door open for the elderly to contact a social worker should the need arise, rather than have the aide attempt to deal with a problem herself.

We could multiply examples of what should or should not be assigned to an aide, and what should remain the responsibility of the social worker. In summary, the aide is not prepared to discuss the emotional implications or reactions of the person to whom she is rendering a tangible service, nor should she be expected to be. While professional supervision is helpful to the aide, it cannot eliminate what appear to be the dangers inherent in such practices. Furthermore, acceptable standards of practice cannot be maintained unless the distinction between professional social work and nonprofessional service is recognized and adhered to.

An outstanding example of the proper use of nonprofessional personnel is the experiment conducted by the Family Service Association of America, supported by a grant from the National Institute of Mental Health, through several of its affiliated family agencies that provided adequate professional supervision. According to a progress report, 185 elderly people were helped by these nonprofessional workers. The elderly had problems with housing, physical and mental health, inadequate income, difficulty in managing income, marital problems, interfamilial relationships, and personal adaptation to the circumstances in which they found themselves. The nonprofessional aides were limited to encouraging and accompanying the elderly to the needed facilities; they served as additional workers concerned about the isolated or depressed person. While it was feared at first that the introduction of another person would impair the professional relationship with the social worker, this proved not to be the case. That relationship was safeguarded by the understanding that as soon as the elderly person evidenced strain or stress, the aide would attempt to motivate him to use the counseling services of the professional workers.

The aides also made contact with community agencies and institutions which could provide services for the elderly. Such contacts are often time-consuming, for which "the professionals never have sufficient time, and which in fact do not require the skills of professionals," as was stated in the report. These contacts not only helped the agencies to increase their knowledge about facilities which could be counted on to provide services for the elderly, but also helped them to become more aware of gaps in services. The experiment also proved, as was so often proved in the past, that personal contact between agencies is useful in establishing better cooperative relationships.

The report indicates that the success of the program was due to the introduction of mature nonprofessionals who were sensitive, warm, and understanding. In training these nonprofessionals, emphasis was put on the need to be aware of signs of stress and to accept responsibility to motivate the elderly to use professional counseling when such signs appeared.

It is evident that considerable stress was laid on maintaining a distinction between professional and nonprofessional personnel by circumscribing the responsibilities of the latter and limiting them to the performance of such duties as were assigned to them. Within these limits, nonprofessional assistance can be effectively utilized to help the elderly.[2]

Such careful limitations, however, are not always imposed nor are they controlled. Experience shows that the pressure of growing need for services and the easy availability of aides has proved conducive, in some instances, to a tendency to substitute the services of the latter for professional intervention in providing help rather than for supplementation of such help. This tendency is understandable if we consider the heavy load which the professional workers are often called upon to carry. The tendency to utilize aides is encouraged both by the need of the professional workers to relieve themselves of a burden and by their desire to retain the help of the aides by attempting to give them more interesting and absorbing tasks. Thus, there develops in some instances the tendency to assign to case aides direct social work responsibility, with the result that professional contact with the elderly person diminishes and may even cease completely, the professional worker confining herself more and more to supervision and consultation. Since both supervision and consultation rank higher than casework practice in the hierarchy of the social work structure, this tactic can be used by the professional as a means of achieving higher status.

In summary, one can say that the way in which the non-

[2] "Social Work Team with Aging Family Service Clients."

professionals are used will determine the value of the practice of employing them. Used as aides to the professional worker, the nonprofessionally trained personnel fill a very important role. In addition to serving the elderly, as well as the organization in which they are employed, the aides—frequently young persons—are exposed to contact with older people, gain a better understanding of their needs, and can serve as interpreters of those needs to the lay community of which they are a part.

One could reasonably assume that the young person so employed and so exposed to the values of social work services would become interested in obtaining professional training. This, however, does not seem to be the case. In some instances, as for example in the experiment conducted by the Family Service Association, the aides are older women who have no desire or intention of securing further training. Even where the aides are younger people, one finds that for them this work is in the nature of a temporary job. Moreover, in addition to the lack of interest in professional training on the part of the aides, there appears to be no attempt to motivate them in that direction.

Despite the fact that the social work profession has long since abandoned the concept that on-the-job training is adequate preparation for future work and instills a recognition of the value of professional training in meeting people's needs, we encounter in some places the argument that nonprofessional personnel can do as well as professionals, provided they have understanding, warmth, and dedication. This would see to negate the value of professional training and take us back to the beginnings of social work, and a step toward jeopardizing standards.

Even more important is the fact that through the em-

ployment of aides to do work formerly done by professionals, we may fail to provide the elderly with the kind
of help they most urgently need, for we shall be concen-
trating on concrete needs and neglecting their deeply seated
emotional problems. One cannot help but question whether
this kind of practice does not indicate a low esteem for the
elderly, and whether an extended policy of employing nonprofessional personnel may not be motivated by financial
considerations rather than by interest in the elderly.

In the course of studying some of the cases handled by
aides, it became apparent that work with family members,
who had indicated their interest in the older person by
bringing his problems to the attention of the agency, is
seldom undertaken. The reason frequently given is again
the fact that relatives do not wish to be involved. Two
questions come to mind. Is it not possible that, under pressure of work, there is reluctance to add to the load by
bringing the relatives into the process? At the same time, is
it not possible that the nonprofessional worker does not
know, nor can she be expected to know, how to involve
the relatives? Another possibility to be considered is that
the relatives, sensing the worker's inexperience, are unwilling to expose their personal problems to her. Whatever the
real reason behind this lack of interest, the fact remains that
by thus isolating the older person, we are contributing to
the rift in family relationships rather than helping to increase the family's participation in the problems of the
elderly.

No criticism of the aides is implied in these statements.
Rather they reflect the inadequate consideration being given
to the assignment of this work and to the relinquishment
of the social worker's responsibility for attention to all as-

pects of the work with the elderly. And yet, the kind of supervision which would keep the social worker in close touch with the problems of the individual is time-consuming. Since the employment of aides is considered justifiable on the basis of relief from caseload pressures, this advantage would be forfeited if supervision of the kind here indicated as essential were to be undertaken.

GROUP COUNSELING

In the past, the one-to-one relationship of the social casework method was the one employed almost exclusively in working with the elderly, as well as with other groups in the population. The pressure of the problems presented by the growing number of elderly, as well as the lack of personnel to handle these problems led to experimentation with the group counseling method which had demonstrated its value in other settings.

The difference between these two methods—casework and group work—is that whereas in the social casework method reliance is placed on the relationship between the caseworker and the individual concerned to arrive at a solution of a problem, the group counseling method places its reliance on the interaction among the group members under the leadership of the group worker. In utilizing this particular method with the elderly it becomes necessary to adapt the traditional group counseling experience to meet the elderly person's particular needs.

Aims of the group. The group is set up partly to provide a socializing experience, so important to many elderly or impaired people. Recognizing how difficult the older person's poor self-image makes it for him to join a group, the first appeal is made on the basis of a social occasion, an opportunity to leave the confines of his home. Consequently, an effort is made to create a pleasant and relaxed atmosphere.

It is recognized that, regardless of its other values, the group can make an important contribution by keeping the elderly person in contact with, and related to, the outside world. It is hoped that the new relationships which he can form through the group will compensate, at least in some measure, for the losses he sustained in the process of aging.

The socializing experience, important as it is in helping to develop new relationships, is only part of the general aim. Some of the goals of the group counseling method which are of particular significance for the elderly are to (1) support personality strength; (2) encourage feelings of self-worth and self-acceptance; (3) promote self-mastery; (4) encourage each participant to take action in his own behalf and work to control his own experiences; and (5) lead toward an increased appreciation of one's own resources and a sense of personal competence, with a release of spontaneity and creativity.[3]

In order for the members of the group to develop their ability to discuss their problems, the leader must help them to feel that they are not alone in experiencing a variety of difficulties, that they are not different or unique, that their concerns are shared by many others. By arousing interest, encouraging discussion, treating each member with respect for his worth and dignity, and providing an atmosphere of freedom, the leader enables the participants to bring up for discussion whatever subject is of interest to them, even if the subject is unpleasant or threatening, such as their fear of death, or is fraught with a great deal of emotional ten-

---

[3] This and some of the other information in the next three paragraphs are taken from Klein *et al.*

sion, such as their feelings of being rejected by their children.

To accomplish this aim, the leader must have the ability to listen, to be attuned to what the members of the group are attempting to say but cannot verbalize. Often, it means that the leader must put into words what a member of the group is implying, and universalize the experience.

Different methods have been devised to encourage discussion when it does not flow easily, such as referring to plays, films, television series, newspaper articles bearing on the subject under discussion, and attempting to elicit the members' reactions. It has also been found helpful to provide information in some areas of the participants' interest when there is indication of lack of familiarity with the subject matter. This helps to broaden perspectives, encourages interest, and at times leads to activities designed to help in a given situation.

Values of a group experience. As the members begin to feel themselves part of the group, and as they are helped to see that any subject of interest to them is a proper subject for discussion, they are encouraged to bring up those matters which are of a special importance to them. These include all areas of living which present particular difficulties for them, including such topics as illness, lack of social contacts, reaction to the need to become dependent, relationship with their children, marital difficulties, feelings relating to their need for privacy and for a sense of dignity.

Through group interaction, the participants often find answers to the many questions which have been troubling them for a long time. There was Mr. M., for instance, who was concerned about his cardiac condition and lack of social contacts, and who found reassurance and friendships through the group. Mrs. S. was eager to maintain her independence, and she found that she could discuss this need and her concern with others whose needs were similar to her own. Mrs. R., becoming convinced that the group members were interested in her, was able to depend less on her daughter for some form of relationship to another person, even though she resented this dependence. These are but a few of the values which the members of one group found through their association with one another.

As was to be expected, there are problems which group members can discuss easily even at the very beginning of the sessions, while in other instances their concerns can be brought out into the open only after they learn to be together and to trust one another. As the members learn to express their feelings and find that their needs are being accepted as valid and that other members have similar problems, their reluctance to expose their inner feelings can be overcome. They begin to see that whatever their problems may be in no way alters their status in the group.

At the same time, sharing their experiences helps to dissipate their loneliness, relieves their anxieties, and they gain strength from the support they receive. They also learn that there are different ways in which individuals handle their problems and they are more inclined to accept variations in adjustment. As the participants learn to question themselves in the same way that they question others, they gain a better understanding of their mistakes in dealing with the situations which confront them. All this is conducive to a better relationship with others from which they can derive support.

As the group members find their place within the group and become active participants rather than being merely listeners, they grow in their feeling of worth and self-esteem, are more comfortable in asserting their right to differ, to discuss, and to defend their point of view, while at the same time showing more appreciation and respect for the views of others. This helps to broaden their vision, improve their tolerance and their ability to give warmth and support to others.

At the same time, they learn to draw strength from their past achievements and discover within themselves qualities of courage and hopefulness. The security which they derive enables them to recognize their problems and modify their behavior.

The group method has thus proved to be a valuable tool in helping the elderly with their personal and social adjustments. It is encouraging to note that social workers are trying new methods of dealing with such problems. We can hope and expect that improvement in the old methods as well as development of new methods will take place as experience and knowledge grow. Whatever developments occur in the future will undoubtedly be geared, as the present methods are geared, to attest to the conviction of social work that we must preserve, sustain, and enrich family life in so far as it is possible to do so.

9. *LOOKING TO THE FUTURE*

Our discussion so far has demonstrated clearly that advanced age in itself need not be a deterrent to the achievement of a satisfying and productive life, but that it is frequently influenced, for better or for worse, by the attitude of society toward the older person. Improvement in the conditions under which the elderly must spend their later years can only come about as society gains a better understanding of the needs of the older person and shows a willingness to provide the facilities to meet these needs.

Slowly the community has come to the realization that aging brings in its wake both personal and social changes. Furthermore, the pressures of these changes not only have a profound effect on the older person, but can help or hinder the maintenance of healthy family relationships.

In our own time, we see an awakened interest in the plight of the elderly, replacing the previously existing disinterest and neglect. We have come a long way in our appreciation of the needs of this group in our population, as well as in our attempts to initiate constructive measures for the improvement of all areas of living. Steps have been taken to improve the income of the elderly, to secure more adequate medical care and housing suitable to their needs, and to provide for the utilization of their free time. Impressive as these achievements are, it is apparent that what has been done so far is not nearly enough for the elderly of today, nor is it geared toward meeting the needs of the elderly of tomorrow.

As a basis for projecting future needs, it is essential to have a clear appreciation of the numbers involved and what might be needed for the solution of existing problems. It is hoped that such an improved understanding might affect in a wholesome way the familial relationship, which has presented such serious problems in the past.

Aging in the Future

The trend toward greater longevity, which began with the decrease in infant mortality and better medical care for all sections of the population, is resulting in the fact that old age is now constituting an ever larger slice of our total life span. More people are reaching, and will continue to reach, what is known as a ripe old age. It has been estimated that the population 65 years of age or older, which now numbers twenty million, is increasing at the rate of some 300,000 a year.

There are numerous studies devoted to statistics relating to the elderly and to every aspect of life as it affects them. Comparisons have been made between the elderly of today and those who might be in that category tomorrow. These comparisons are related to age, sex, living arrangements, medical conditions, and the many other characteristics of the aged population which can be illustrated through statistics.

It seems unnecessary to go into these statistics here. It does not require any close analysis to demonstrate that the thirty million people over 65 years of age (which studies project as being the probable number at the end of this century) will be totally different from the comparatively small number—slightly over 2,800,000—who comprised the aged population at the beginning of the century.

The implications of these figures are obvious. The elderly of today have lived through a variety of economic, social, and technological changes, and consequently the world in which they live is totally different from the world which awaits the elderly of tomorrow. How different this coming world will be, can best be appreciated by a backward glance at our society of yesteryear. We are now witnessing a technological revolution which could not be envisioned even a short few years ago. The effect of these changes on our way of life is underscored as we consider the widespread use of computers, the walk on the moon, and the projected landing on Mars. The young men of today, who have learned to accept these miracles of science as everyday occurrences, who will be the old men in the year 2000, will be very different from the old men of 1900, or even of 1970. They will be retiring earlier, and because of this youthfulness, the retired—meaning aging—men of tomorrow will have different needs, and their demands for the satisfaction of these needs will be different.

As we view present-day measures for meeting the needs of the elderly, we are impressed by the fact that they were made piecemeal and that they remain inadequate to enable the elderly to share on an equal basis in our affluent society. The laws so far passed grant only niggardly allowances. This

is due partly to the fact that the elderly continue to be regarded as second-class citizens; partly it is due to a lack of
knowledge about the aged and the process of aging. Much
more will need to be known than we know now. This lack
of knowledge and understanding was pointed out by Dr.
D. B. Bromley, a member of the psychology staff of the
University of Liverpool, England, who stated: "We spend
a quarter of our lives growing up and three quarters growing
old. It is strange, therefore, that psychologists and others
have devoted most of their efforts to the study of childhood
and adolescence." [1]

It is to be hoped that in the future more attention will be
directed to understanding what the elderly require. Let us
consider what measures will be necessary to enable the elderly to achieve status and a full participation in the life
around them. Any future planning must take into consideration the fact that the difficulties which the elderly encounter
are multidimensional and that no single method can be devised to meet them all. The list of National Objectives for
Older Americans, as set forth in the Older Americans Act,
points out clearly what should be done:

Equal opportunity for the full and free enjoyment of the
following:

An adequate income in retirement in accordance with the
American standard of living.

The best possible physical and mental health which science
can make available without regard to economic status.

Suitable housing, independently selected, designed and located
with reference to special needs and available at costs which
older citizens can afford.

Full restorative services for those who require institutional
care.

[1] Bromley, p. 13.

Opportunity for employment with no discriminatory personnel practices because of age.

Retirement to health, honor and dignity after years of contribution to the economy.

Pursuit of meaningful activity, within the widest range of civic, cultural and recreational opportunities.

Efficient community services which provide social assistance in a coordinated manner and which are readily available when needed.

Immediate benefit from proven research knowledge which can sustain and improve health and happiness.

Freedom, independence and the free exercise of individual initiative in planning and managing their own lives.[2]

These objectives encompass the whole gamut of needs in every area of the older person's daily existence. It is obvious that they cannot all be accomplished at once, or in the immediate future. The very fact, however, that they have been enumerated in detail in the National Objectives draws attention to the wide gap now existing between the needs and the necessary services.

Many of the recommendations have as yet not been implemented. Thus, in the report of the President's Task Force on Aging—"Toward a Better Future for the Elderly," released in June, 1970, some five years later—we find many of the same recommendations, on which action is still pending.[3]

Needed Steps to Economic Betterment

We have witnessed the slow pace of measures for improving the economic status of the elderly, from the first inadequate

[2] Older Americans Act of 1965, p. 1.

[3] "Presidential Task Force on Aging Urges Action Now to Help Elderly," p. 4.

assistance on the local level to the assumption of this responsibility by the federal government, which culminated in the passage of the Social Security Act and the introduction of amendments from time to time to rectify inadequacies.

Even the latest increases in social security benefits, granted in 1971, encouraging as they are, still fall short of actual requirements, failing, as in previous years, to keep pace with the cost of living. An important drawback toward achieving more realistic benefits may be accounted for by the fact that increases in social security benefits appear to have been tied to political considerations in the past as undoubtedly they will be in the future. Living costs, however, continue to climb. The net result is that many of the elderly continue to require supplementation to meet their essential needs, whether this supplementation comes from their children or through private or public agencies.

There is evidence to indicate that the legislators have been aroused sufficiently to recognize the inadequacy of the present-day grants and the necessity for change. For instance, in one move to raise social security benefits, there was incorporated a proposal for an automatic adjustment of benefits to the cost of living. Though this was voted down, there is nevertheless reason to believe that social security grants will continue to rise in the future and that some of the restrictions will be removed. Whether these changes will be adequate to meet the ever escalating cost of living and thus assure for the elderly an old age of security and dignity, remains to be seen.

There are, in addition, other factors which will influence, for better or for worse, the future financial condition of the elderly.

On the positive side, it can be assumed that the opportunity for a large number of hitherto disadvantaged young people to achieve a higher educational level will be reflected in a better earning capacity which will give them a broader base for the computation of their social security benefits as well as allow a margin of saving for their retirement years. One can also assume with reasonable certainty that the number of workers who will receive private pensions upon retirement will be greater as time goes on. This will help to supplement their social security benefits and their savings.

On the other hand, one must recognize that despite these measures the income of the elderly may continue to lag behind rising living costs. In fact, the economic insufficiency of the older part of the population may become even more serious as industrial developments proceed at a more rapid pace, as the need for new skills becomes more frequently felt, and as retirement occurs at earlier ages.

The lengthened life span and the shortened working period may continue to impose a heavy burden on the working part of the population, affecting adversely their ability to provide for their own old age. The situation is further complicated by the fact that both the lengthened life span and earlier retirement may mean that the working person will face the problem of extending financial assistance not to one but to two generations of unemployed old relatives.

RECENT PROPOSALS

Appreciation of the gravity of the older person's situation has led within recent years to a variety of proposals designed to alleviate their plight.

As far back as 1968, the former Secretary of the Department of Health, Education, and Welfare, Wilbur J. Cohen, advocated the establishment of a federally financed system of income payments. This was followed by the introduction of a bill in the United States Senate to guarantee an annual income for the elderly. In introducing this bill, Wilson L. Prouty, Republican Senator from Vermont, not only emphasized the inadequacy of social security benefits, but pointed to the fact that some of the elderly are excluded from benefits because of lack of coverage during their working years. The social security benefits of those whose wages were low, he mentioned are of course quite insufficient.

While Senator Prouty's proposal of an annual income is woefully inadequate—$1200 a year for a single person and $1800 for a couple—and would leave many elderly to continue to function below the poverty level, nevertheless it is a significant proposal which points to an awakening recognition of the extent of the need and a conviction that more than the present benefits are necessary.

Members of the Congress and leaders of the public, have expressed their endorsement of the need for instituting more adequate measures recognizing that merely the adjustment of benefits to the cost of living is not enough. The importance of guaranteeing an adequate annual income for the elderly, as it is for others of the poor of our population, is receiving more acceptance. The recent proposal of a Family Assistance Plan embodies this concept of a satisfactory income level for the poor segment of our population, including the needy elderly. It is recognized that the adoption of such a measure would go a long way in assuring some degree of security in old age. At the same time, it would relieve the middle-aged working population of the burden of having to supplement the income of the elderly, thus allowing them to plan more effectively for their own retirement.

So far, the blind adherence to the practice of mandating

retirement at a given age hurts not only the individual worker, but the employer and society as a whole. Both the employer and society lose the accumulated knowledge and skills while disregarding the possibility of adapting such skills to the present-day requirements of a particular job, or changing the job specifications to fit the worker's capabilities. In addition, the cost of training new workers imposes an additional financial burden on the employer, which is eventually reflected in higher costs to the consumer.

Both the practice of mandatory retirement and the inadequate income of the elderly contribute immeasurably to the erosion in family relationships which is likely to occur even when the responsibility for the care of the older person is undertaken by the younger generation voluntarily. That such dependence affects adversely both the giver and the receiver of help has been demonstrated repeatedly.

Need for Improved Medical Care

It is generally recognized that adequate medical care ranks with economic security as one of the most important needs of the elderly. As yet, there are no programs of care that meet either the preventive or the therapeutic needs of this group. In addition, there is a lack of adequate planning for the efficient distribution of services.

It is, of course, difficult to predict what the medical requirements of the aged will be in the future. It can be reasonably assumed that continued advances in medical science will eliminate many of the diseases which now plague the elderly. At the same time, increased longevity may well bring to the fore a number of ailments and disabilities for which medicine has as yet not discovered a cure. Regardless of the particular diagnostic categories we are likely to encounter in the years to come, there is little question that both prevention and therapy, as well as healthful nutrition, will play an important role in forestalling and treating the ills of the elderly. It has been demonstrated, for instance, that preventive measures, which in the past were considered to be inapplicable to the elderly, are now becoming more widely accepted and have proved their worth in detecting abnormalities which could have led to more serious complications.

We are also becoming aware that other areas of the person's life have an important bearing on his health as age advances. Studies have indicated the close correlation which exists between the economic condition of the individual and his ability or inability to secure medical care. For care, or the lack of it, may result in the absence or presence of serious illness in later life. Similarly, proper nutrition, adequate housing and some form of useful work have by their availability or lack of it an important bearing on the health of the elderly person and, therefore, must be considered an integral and indispensable part of any program of preventive care for the aged.

This more recent view of what is meant as prevention, in all its aspects, sharply points up the need to recognize the importance of the whole climate of the individual's life if early preventive measures are to be undertaken long before actual old age sets in.

ENACTED LEGISLATION

The use of therapeutic facilities has been perceptibly greater within recent years since the passage of the Medicare and

Medicaid laws. The benefits which Medicare brings to the elderly can be judged by the numbers who have taken advantage of the program by seeking hospital care for the treatment of long-neglected conditions, as well as by the numbers who have subscribed for the voluntary insurance protection which is embodied in the Medicare law. Here too, however, one can discern the effect of the economic condition of the individual and the amount of coverage he can secure. It has been shown that the percentage of elderly in the low-income group who took advantage of the insurance is below that of the rest of the population.

Recognizing the importance of the economic factor, Wilbur J. Cohen, former Secretary of Health, Education, and Welfare, has advocated in his "Action Line for Aging," previously referred to, the need for "putting the entire Medicare program on a social insurance prepayment basis, specifically to combine the medical insurance and hospital insurance parts of Medicare and finance both from social insurance contributions and matching contributions from the Federal Government." [4]

The inadequacies of Medicare are receiving considerable attention, and specific recommendations for the inclusion of presently omitted services have been made repeatedly. Attention to these deficiencies will, it is to be hoped, lead to revision.

It is hoped that in the future more attention will be given to insure better medical care for the elderly, eliminating the present lacks in hospitals, nursing homes, and other types of institutions. As things now stand, there appears to be incontrovertible truth in the statement made with reference to nursing homes that "most . . . are persistent, though silent

[4] Cohen, p. 17.

and well-hidden evidence that we still do not take the care of the aged seriously." [5]

So far as the home care programs are concerned, this would involve more extensive use of a variety of home health aids than is possible at present. Even more important is the need to recognize that family members who would have the major responsibility for the care of the patient in the home would need a great deal of support to combat the distress to which they are frequently subjected as they witness the suffering and deterioration of their elderly relative. This is particularly true because the strain imposed by the situation is not of a passing nature, but is likely to continue over prolonged periods of time.

There has developed recently an appreciation of the fact that improvement in the care of the elderly, as well as of the rest of the population, lies in removing the economic burden of such care through a compulsory health insurance program, whether such a program be financed through the social security system or by joint effort of the federal government and private funds. Whatever form it will eventually take, it is felt that it will be beneficial since it will affirm the right of every citizen to health and medical care.

INADEQUACIES IN THE DELIVERY OF SERVICES

The frequently inadequate medical care provided for the elderly is further aggravated by the poor distribution of such services within the community.

The increased specialization in medicine, which was brought about by the expansion of medical knowledge, has led to the shuttling of patients from one physician to another and from one clinic to another on the basis of the particular disease

[5] Friedman and Coleman, p. 213.

entity or even the particular complaint made by the patient. While the patient who is attended by a private physician can rely on the latter to correlate the findings of the various specialists to whom he is being referred, the patient who attends a clinic has no one to assume this responsibility in a great many instances. As a result, all too often, the importance of some pathological condition may be overlooked and remain untreated.

What is true of any clinic patient is doubly true of the older patient, whose very age is frequently an important factor in the failure to arouse interest and concern. This is particularly significant since the medical picture of the older person is often complex, and failure to correlate the findings of different specialists can have grave consequences.

An understanding of all these factors makes it apparent that there is need for some drastic changes in the system of delivery of services. Studies of the less prosperous sections of the community have revealed two important factors which emphasize the need for such changes, namely: (1) The elderly person frequently seeks medical attention only when his illness has reached a crisis. In fact, many people in the underprivileged communities, but especially the elderly, have no contact with a physician except in a crisis situation. (2) Treatment of disease, we now know, can no longer be regarded as the exclusive province of the physician in his one-to-one relationship with his patient, but becomes the shared responsibility of a number of other professionals whose understanding of the various aspects of the patient's life situation can make a significant contribution to the total medical picture and, consequently, can have a bearing on the rendering of appropriate medical care and thus on his health and welfare.

This appreciation of the various factors which must be taken into consideration so far as the health of all the community residents is concerned, led to the establishment of community health centers, the staffs of which include not only medical specialists, but public health nurses and social workers as well, all working as a team. The success of these centers emphasizes the need to reach out into the community in order to discover those individuals who are, on the whole, nonusers of medical services rather than wait for them to seek a physician at a time of crisis. The elderly comprise a large section of the nonusers in a community, and it is hoped that the goal of reaching out into the community and discovering the nonusers in it will have beneficial effects on the elderly as well. By such active exploration of the health needs of a community, the community centers perform not only a therapeutic service, but a vastly important preventive one. It is hoped that expansion of these centers will proceed apace.

MEETING THE NEEDS OF THE MENTALLY ILL

Development of facilities for meeting the needs of the mentally ill elderly has proceeded at an even slower pace than was the case where the physically ill elderly were concerned. What appears to have stood in the way of progress is the fear of mental illness in all its forms, even the milder forms of mental disorder, which still persists among many segments of the lay community. More important, however, has been the lack of interest on the part of many members of the medical profession and the lack of conviction that worthwhile results can be obtained from intensive therapy. Some comfort can be derived from the demonstration that innovative techniques are producing favorable results. As an illustration one might cite a recently developed technique named "crisis therapy," a form of group therapy, which was conducted at the Bronx (New York) State Mental Hospital with a group of twelve patients who had been diagnosed as "psychotic."

This group met weekly. The goal was to reduce tension by allowing them to express their anger and other feelings which they considered to be inadmissible, to alleviate their guilt, to examine their fears, and to help them accept reality. By the end of six months of treatment in group sessions, all twelve patients were discharged from the hospital and returned to community living.

According to the group leader:

In not one instance was the State Mental Hospital the end of the road for these patients. . . . Yet at the outset they were virtually indistinguishable from the typically confused and disoriented patient who is usually considered hopeless, and whose diagnosis of organicity usually precludes psychotherapy of the type we found so effective.[6]

Another kind of experimental treatment was conducted with a group of patients suffering from severe depression at the Veterans Administration Hospital in Tuscaloosa, Alabama. This was a type of attitude therapy known as "kind firmness." It was begun in 1962 and has been continued ever since. The purpose of the therapy was to give the patient ample opportunity to express his hostility. He was assigned a simple task and was held rigidly to a perfect performance. He was not offered help when he was unable to complete the task, but he was not ridiculed or belittled because of it. Once he was able to express his anger, he was taken off the program.

An evaluation of the program under strictly controlled

[6] Oberleder, p. 6.

conditions showed that "this therapeutic device is superior to anything else available for the treatment of depression." Following treatment, the patients "had a more positive self-concept and manifested improved interpersonal relationships with family members and others. The results were superior to those achieved through other forms of treatment." [7]

The demonstrated effectiveness of these two innovative approaches leads one to hope that not only will they be adopted in other settings, but that other new approaches may be attempted in the future. It is important to keep in mind, however, that these are only experiments, even though they are fruitful experiments, and that no carefully worked out plan for the treatment of the mentally ill has as yet been devised. It has been said of the community mental health centers that they are disorganized, disjointed, antiquated, obsolete nonsystems of health care.

Although there is a growing conviction that the state mental hospital is not a satisfactory place for the elderly mentally ill, the number of patients who have been discharged to such other facilities as nursing homes or homes for the aged is very limited indeed. Nor do we have a valid follow-up system to indicate the kind of adjustment these patients have achieved.

The conviction that the mentally ill elderly patient is now consigned to a state mental hospital merely because nothing else is available, led to the adoption of screening procedures to eliminate those elderly who might be kept out of these institutions. Such a project was undertaken by the California Department of Mental Health, under the name of the Geriatric Screening Project. A report states that of "161 patients screened during the first half of 1968, only two percent were

7 Folsom, pp. 1 and 5.

committed, six percent were placed in boarding homes, sixteen percent in county and private general hospitals, eighteen percent in nursing homes. The majority, (fifty-eight percent) remained at home, with the help of supportive services." [8]

Similar screening projects for patients awaiting admission to state mental hospitals were undertaken in a number of other localities. Those patients whose problems were physical in origin or in the area of financial inadequacy or social maladaptation were screened out and referred to other agencies in the community equipped to handle them.

At the same time, attempts have been made to institute intensive treatment, both for newly admitted patients as well as for patients who had been in the hospital for a number of years. The results indicated that in both categories there was marked improvement in many instances, resulting in an earlier return to the community than could have been accomplished had such treatment not been available.

Such experimentation with new approaches and the satisfactory results so obtained point the way toward improved care for the mentally ill elderly.

A well-coordinated plan whose objective was to avoid permanent isolation of the mentally ill elderly in a mental hospital was devised in Israel, where the aged with mental disturbances created a very serious problem. A psychiatric geriatric ward was opened as an addition to one of the hospitals located near a home for the aged, where all the diagnostic and rehabilitation facilities were available to the mentally disturbed aged. The following arrangements were offered:

1. A day hospital to serve the aged from surrounding homes for the aged. This service offers a group of aged special attention

[8] "Psychiatric Screening of Geriatric Patients." p. 3.

from the psychiatric team through group therapy and occupational therapy.

2. A halfway house not far from the hospital and within the framework of the home for the aged. Here, the aged who have completed treatment in the psychiatric geriatric ward are transferred until their final discharge to their regular environment. They continue under supervision of the psychiatric team while here.

3. A long-stay annex for patients with severe mental deterioration who require supervision of the psychiatric-geriatric team of the hospital, but who do not require hospital care, and cannot remain within the environs of the home for the aged.

4. An outpatient clinic for disturbed aged.

5. Follow-up service in which a psychiatric nurse and a social worker visit the homes for the aged under supervision of the psychiatrist. They work with the staffs there and offer supportive treatment for discharged patients.[9]

It is pointed out that:

This multiple approach has led to abandonment of the previous tendency to label as senile dementia every aged person with a mental disturbance. . . . We attempt to determine each aged disturbed person's capabilities and our care is directed to preparing him for the social role most suitable for him at this stage of his life. At the same time, we prepare the family or others in his environment to which he will be discharged to be more understanding and tolerant. Even for those with severe mental deterioration, an attempt is made to help the patient manage the elementary daily activities of living by conditioning. . . . Over one half of the patients discharged after treatment were able to return to their own or a substitute home.[10]

In our own country too, an attempt is being made to urge a more coordinated and thoroughgoing plan of care for the mentally ill. In its report on the elderly and the state

[9] Margulec, pp. 252–53.   [10] *Ibid.*, p. 253.

mental hospital, the Community Service Society of New York points out that "to place aged patients in a State Hospital unless it is necessary and clearly indicated is a shocking and inhuman error for all concerned." The report, submitted to Governor Nelson A. Rockefeller urging prompt action, outlined a six-point program:

1. Establishment of a network of community-based geriatric centers, each serving a definite area, to provide diagnosis, short-term treatment and placement.

2. Development of small residential units specializing in long-term care of the mildly confused, ambulatory elderly persons.

3. Expansion of and broadened services by nursing homes and infirmaries. These could be special facilities, infirmary sections of homes for the aged, city or county infirmaries, or specialized sections of State mental hospitals.

4. Public housing for the aged should be expanded broadly and provide comprehensive services for elderly tenants.

5. State mental hospitals should be strengthened as one of the elements in the services for the elderly program, with increased emphasis on medical service.

6. Legislation should be passed providing for appointment of a conservator of the property of an elderly person during the period when he may be temporarily unable to handle his daily responsibilities.[11]

Both the Geriatric Screening Project and the report from Israel emphasize the necessity of supportive services to family members or others who must deal with whatever adjustment difficulties the mildly disturbed elderly person may continue to manifest long after he is considered as no longer needing psychiatric care. It is to be hoped that any comprehensive plan for the care of the mentally disabled aged

[11] "Six-Point Program Urged in New York State for Dependent Aging," p. 16.

will include such supportive services to families. It is important to acknowledge that, so far, no adequate plan has been devised to help families to cope more successfully and with greater ease with the problems which they encounter.

The success of such a plan can be assured only as we recognize more clearly the impact of the problems with which the families of mentally ill patients—no matter how minimal the disturbance—are called upon to meet. Into these problems go all the disquieting reactions we have been discussing in relation to caring for physically ill persons. Because of these difficulties, families to whom mentally ill patients are to be returned, must be chosen with a great deal of care. It must be ascertained that they have the strength necessary to withstand the difficulties which they are bound to encounter; that they have sufficient love for the patient, and that they have the ability to learn to understand his problem, as well as how to care for him. Given all these conditions, plus supportive services and continued medical supervision, many of the elderly now languishing in state mental hospitals could be returned to the community. Despite the advances made so far, it is admitted that much more needs to be done to improve services for the mentally ill elderly, which, it has often been pointed out, are disorganized and frequently suffer from insufficient financing. Most important drawback to adequate care, however, is the lack of interest in, and concern for, this group.

What is needed is a concerted effort to eradicate the misconception that mental illness of the elderly and its effects cannot be altered and that, therefore, there is presumably no need for elaborate medical care. If a changed attitude on the part of the community could be achieved, it would soon be reflected in a changed attitude on the part of the medical personnel, whose interest could be enlisted to provide better facilities and care for these patients. Such manifestation of interest would be conducive to an acceptance of the individual, regardless of his age, and of his right to such care as would restore him to maximal functioning and participation in social relationships.

At the same time, it would have a beneficial effect on family members who carry the major responsibility for the patient. As they see that the older person's condition is considered important by his physician and other professional personnel, they would feel that they are not carrying an insupportable burden alone.

Improvement in Living Arrangements

All the losses which are sustained by the elderly in the process of aging have an important bearing on the pattern of living suitable for them. The urban community, where the majority of elderly live, is patently ill-suited to their needs. The tempo of city life, the constant stream of rapidly moving traffic, the wide one-way streets—all impede the mobility of older people. Frequently, they are unable to take advantage of such recreational and cultural activities which are afforded by the city. The neighborliness which exists in small towns and in the rural communities is practically non-existent.

There is evidence of a growing trend to attempt to mitigate some of these difficulties by means of living quarters adapted to the needs of the older person. As yet, however, there is no unanimity as to what is the most desirable type of facility. The fact is that one cannot generalize as to what is best for the aged as a group; the elderly differ, as do the rest of us, and no single solution can meet the needs of all.

In discussing possible future housing needs, one article points out that within the next sixteen years, Americans will have to work only six months in a year to maintain the standard of living they now enjoy, and that they may retire at the unbelievable age of 38. Because their interests will be different from those of the retired people of today, the director of the California Study of Retirement Housing suggests the development of an "urban campus concept which would provide a full complement of needed facilities and which would keep retired people within the mainstream of American culture." The facilities and services of such a campus would be available to the surrounding community, thus avoiding segregation. The author states that since many features of the campus are already incorporated in today's retirement centers, "perhaps we have taken the first major steps toward providing a meaningful and happy retirement for all Americans.[12]

Regardless of the type of residence which the elderly consider suitable at the beginning of the period known as "old age," their needs often change with advancing years. The possibility of such changes and the frequently encountered strong reaction to change of residence must be taken into account when planning for the future. It is hoped that it may be possible to have residences in which the elderly can move from one part to another in accordance with their needs at any particular time.

The prototype of such an arrangement is the Isabella Home in New York City. It contains accommodations for the well elderly who can take complete care of themselves; for others

[12] Ledgerwood, pp. 21 and 23.

who may need some form of supervision as well as community cooking facilities; and for still another group, who require infirmary care. The residents can be moved from one part of the home to the other in accordance with the state of their health and their ability to care for themselves at any particular time. Such moves can be arranged on a permanent or temporary basis, and the residents can be returned to their previous living quarters when no other type of care is necessary.

Satisfying Leisure Time

Regardless of advanced years, the older individual remains a member of society and must play a role in it. Having given up, whether voluntarily or involuntarily, his role as a worker he must look for avenues for meaningful use of his time, and not merely to "kill time." Only in this way can he achieve a significant position in society. The achievement of this objective requires adaptations which may be difficult at times. Without such adaptation, retirement is likely to create a feeling of uselessness which is deterimental to the individual's mental health.

The problem is not new, as demonstrated by the attempts made to find recreational and educational opportunities for retired people. Moreover, it is reasonable to assume that it will increase rather than diminish. The reason is twofold: (1) The trend toward much earlier retirement means that more people will have more years of free time after leaving their jobs. It has been estimated, for instance, that in the near future many people can look forward to more than fifteen or twenty years in retirement. (2) Not only retired people, but many of the working population as well will be faced with the need to occupy more hours away from their job as a result of a discernible trend toward a shorter work week. It has been variously estimated that by the year 2000, the average work week will be thirty-one hours, and there are some instances where the four-day, forty-hour week is now in effect.

In view of the expected increase in the number of retired individuals, it seems important to embark now on careful planning for the future. "The great cohort of relatively 'youthful' retirees may pioneer one of the greatest shifts in the history of mankind: the transition from a work-oriented to a leisure-oriented society." [13] Any such planning must take into consideration the fact that the retired people of the years ahead will be better educated, that they will have more sophisticated skills and wider interests than is true of retirees today. Their requirements, so far as ways of using free time is concerned, will be as different from the requirements of today's elderly as the requirements of the latter are different from those of the elderly for whom the first recreational activities were organized.

It is being recognized ever more clearly that what is needed to assure an old age of satisfaction and dignity is productive, creative leisure. As was pointed out: "To the degree that older people remain unprepared for the free time ahead, they will have to be kept busy, distracted, and entertained in order to avoid serious maladaptations. Only preparedness can bring about a full realization of their creative potential." [14] The importance for the need for preparation for the free years ahead cannot be overstressed.

The meaning of the free time has been defined as follows:

[13] Ewald, p. 2.   [14] Martin and Slater, p. 164.

"It must be (1) desired by the individual; (2) socially 'honored,' i.e., without loss of prestige or status; (3) supported by adequate income; and (4) enjoyed at a high level of health." [15] Thus, not only must older people be prepared for free time, but society too must be prepared by creating the conditions which make the enjoyment of what has been called "truly free time" possible.

The type of preparation for retirement which is now being offered by some employers centers primarily on discussing ways to augment or budget retirement income, or on providing information about their rights under the various governmental and pension provisions. Such preparation satisfies some of the workers. It fails, however, to prepare them to make the most of their free time. Only in arriving at a fruitful use of their new-found leisure will the retirees be able to overcome the feelings of frustration and utter uselessness as they are removed from the world of work and from the mainstream of human activities. These deeply seated emotional problems cannot be solved by merely giving information preceding retirement. They must be attacked long before retirement age appears on the horizon, and in an entirely different way, as Dr. Alexander Reid Martin and Dr. Ralph Slater indicate.

New Roles

Unfortunately, most of the retired people of today have had no opportunity to develop their potentials. What these retired elderly people need is an opportunity to continue in some form of work which will capitalize on their accum-

[15] Ewald, *op. cit.*

ulated experience, knowledge, wisdom, and skill so that they may maintain their status in society. The rapid success of the project SERVE, mentioned previously, demonstrates the importance to older people of being able to use their accumulated wisdom and skill. Organized in March, 1966, when 22 retired persons enlisted as volunteers, the organization numbered 564 in 1971. The increase was due mostly to the enthusiastic volunteers themselves who enlisted many of their friends.

Such examples of the fruitful use of the older person's capabilities are few and far between. With few exceptions, most of the employment which is secured, bears little resemblance to the meaningful life from which he was peremptorily removed.

We must accept the fact that we have not yet succeeded in defining and developing significant roles for the older population. This may be due to lack of knowledge of how this can be accomplished. More important, however, is society's unwillingness to acknowledge the older person's ability to make a contribution and, consequently, a lack of flexibility in adapting existing organizations so as to enable the older person to demonstrate what he can do.

Perhaps some help in determining what roles would be considered significant by the older person himself can be found from a pilot study conducted by the Department of Mental Health in California. It points to the fact that the aging individual involved in assessing his life situation often refers to the "attainment or unattainment of life goals." [16] In determining significant roles for an older person, an understanding of his life goals could be of great help, even though admittedly the goals of youth cannot be the goals of old age

[16] Brisette, p. 11.

without some modification. This knowledge, however, could serve as a jumping-off point to help the elderly define what goals would provide satisfaction to them at this time of their life with due regard for such changes as aging produces.

Achievement of Coexistence

Of all the losses sustained by the elderly, whether it be loss of economic self-sufficiency, of physical strength and mental acuity, or even the loss of a significant role in life, none is harder for them to bear than the loss of a satisfactory relationship with the younger members of their families. This loss often assumes a special, even a primary importance. At the same time, the difficulties and inadequacies confronting the elderly often have an adverse effect on the younger generation, as our discussion has pointed out.

As one surveys the realities of life, one cannot deny the existence of a "generation gap" in many instances. Nevertheless, this does not mean that the younger generation is insensitive and unresponsive to the difficulties endured by their elderly relatives. What may often appear to be lack of sympathy may be but the reaction of the young relatives to the heavy emotional burden imposed on them by the need to witness suffering and deterioration. Frustrated and overwhelmed by their helplessness, and the guilt which is often associated with it, they may react with irritability and may even have a desire to run away from an intolerable situation. At other times, the root of the difficulties may be a lack of effective communication between the old and the young, for the two generations view aging and all it implies from different vantage points.

On the whole, it would appear that when the relationship between the older person and his children has been a good and warm one, it is likely to stand up under the impact of the often serious difficulties and strains. If there is understanding of what the children as well as the elderly suffer and a willingness to provide relief from the burden, it may go a long way toward smoothing the situation.

As the span of life lengthens, the two—or even three—generations will have more years to live with each other. Family unity may be disrupted at times by difficulties over which neither generation has any control, and they may need help in reestablishing stability, restoring mutual confidence and respect, and thus preventing permanent injury and premature disintegration of the family.

In order to establish an atmosphere where coexistence is possible, we need what some have called a "generation mix" to counteract the generation gap. Dr. E. M. Bluestone has outlined the problem in this way:

The way to the magic word coexistence must be sought however hard the road. The tendency, or temptation, to condone early separation in home life and elsewhere should be controlled, in order to preserve the integrity of the society in which we must all live. . . . It has become too easy for a family to shake off its aged members when its younger members, in their ambition to thrust forward without restraint, want them out of the way.[17]

In order to achieve this eminently desirable goal, it may be necessary to involve the young and the old, working together, in planning and implementing ways and means of handling the many problems which confront both genera-

[17] Bluestone, "The Growing Impact of Longer Years on Society—a Salute to Youth and a Plea," p. 41.

tions. In becoming thus involved, the young will, it is hoped, begin to appreciate not only the deprivations and stresses which aging imposes, but also the courage which the elderly so often exhibit in the face of almost insuperable odds as well as their sustained ability to think for themselves and make wise decisions.

If changes in the conditions of life of the elderly are to occur, society—and that means the young as well as the old —must be helped to recognize the need for a more positive acceptance of the older generation, a more thorough appreciation of their past contributions and of their value as individuals regardless of their frailty and dependence. The motto of Old Williamsburg, "That the future may learn from the past," could serve as a useful guide to society's attitude toward the elderly.

Future Role of Social Work

We have concentrated on the need for more adequate provisions to meet the deprivations which aging imposes on the individual in the various areas of living. The accomplishment of this goal becomes the task of the various helping professions, and social work, as one of these professions, has an important role to play in the attainment of this objective.

Social work brings to the problems of the older people considerable experience in helping people in trouble. As part of the acquisition of this experience, social workers have learned that the saying "man does not live by bread alone" is more than a chiché; that, in fact, it expresses an important truth about the inner needs of human beings both in their feelings about themselves as individuals and in their relationship to others. Realization of this need has led to an understanding of the importance of helping to organize the kind of services which would make the life of the elderly not only more endurable, but also more meaningful for them. In other words, social work must interpret the need for adequate services in whatever area of life the need arises— economic self-maintenance; satisfactory medical facilities; suitable living quarters; as well as the need of facilities for satisfying use of free time. The reason underlying this responsibility rests upon the fact that *every one* of these problems is a social welfare problem and therefore falls within the sphere of social work activity.

So far, however, social work has failed to meet the challenge which these problems pose. The effect of this failure to improve significantly the position of the elderly in our society is seen in the following statement by the Commissioner on Aging:

These old people not only have the least income. They have the poorest health, the least education, the fewest jobs, the worst housing, and the fewest facilities for frugal, decent living. They are crowded into our core cities, and in most of our core cities their numbers far exceed the proportion of older people in the total population.[18]

Failure persists despite the fact that the skills and attitudes which the social work profession has developed in the process of helping other age groups in our society can be fruitfully applied to the elderly as well. It demands, however, a willingness to exercise some flexibility, essential in meeting the needs of the elderly, as well as readiness to participate actively in drives to promote action to enhance their dignity and self-

[18] Martin, "New Commissioner on Aging Gives Priority to Health, Housing, Jobs," p. 26.

respect. In addition, social work could help to deal more effectively with prejudicial attitudes which have presented such an impenetrable barrier to a satisfactory relationship between the generations.

An important step in assuring adequate services to solve the problems of the elderly would involve the ability to discern problems before they reach a point of crisis, the time when these problems usually come to the attention of social agencies. We have learned through experience that the elderly are too often reluctant to ask for help, since such a request carries with it the implication of their inability to continue their previous independent status—an admission which is too painful for the older individual to accept. As problems are brought to the social worker at a point of crisis, they confront her with the end result of years of deprivation, irremediable erosion of self-sufficiency, and consequently little opportunity for creative intervention, except to meet the presenting need. This recognition of the reluctance to ask for help has led to acceptance of the necessity of locating the "high-risk" elderly, and doing it in such a way as to protect the sensitivities of the elderly.

An example of such "reaching out" is seen in the program adopted by the Old Age Center of the Worcester, Massachusetts, area. The Center organized a two-week campaign through the communication media to notify people that a Center bus would be touring the area. At each bus stop, there was a poster announcing its arrival. Banners at the side of the bus read, "Age Center on the Move—Welcome Aboard."

The original intent was to enlist older people who might be eligible for volunteer work. In this, the project proved successful and served as confirmation of the well-known fact that the elderly wish to be and can be useful workers. At the same time, "the experience . . . convinced the staff of the value of taking an agency to the people." Many who would not have made the trip to the Age Center in downtown Worcester, asked for help with problems. Some of them had not known of the Center and its services; others were reluctant to approach a social agency, or timid about asking questions; some simply had a transportation problem. "The bus was both accessible and sociable."

In some instances, the social worker who talked to the people in private was able to handle a problem on the spot; in other instances, referral was made to the appropriate agency. Not only was it possible in this way to learn of the needs of the elderly but, as the report states, the workers "saw and felt, more directly than ever before, some of the concerns of the elderly citizens and families." It was felt that the experiment brought significant results beyond expectations.[19]

A somewhat different approach is reported from England. Everyone over 75 years of age, in the counties involved in the experiment received a letter from the welfare committee asking the recipient whether he required help of any kind. A prepaid postcard was enclosed for their reply. The needs were tabulated according to priorities, and arrangements were made for volunteers to visit the people to secure more detailed information. Welfare personnel then got in touch with all those who needed help.[20]

These are but two approaches which have proved successful in discovering the needs of the elderly before an emer-

[19] "A Center Takes Its Program to the People—with Results Above Expectations," p. 7.
[20] "Independence for the Aged," p. 1014.

gency situation arises. Other means of achieving the same result can undoubtedly be devised, depending upon the situation in the community under consideration. The indispensable factor in any plan would be the interest of the community in discovering people in need of help and its willingness to provide the necessary services.

The willingness to reach out to find the elderly who need care, the provision of such services as may be indicated, the ability to cope with the multiplicity of difficult problems encountered, particularly with the destructive family relationships, while maintaining a nonjudgmental, helpful attitude toward both the older and the younger generation—perhaps the most difficult problem of all—require appropriate training and a willingness to be flexible in methods and techniques. What is needed above all is an understanding heart as well as a scientific head.

RESPONSIBILITY OF PROFESSIONAL SCHOOLS OF SOCIAL WORK

Until now, schools of social work have, in the main not been in the forefront of the fight for the rights of the elderly to the same extent that is being given to younger age groups. The same attitude often prevails in schools of medicine. Emphasis on the problems of the elderly is still minimal, and priorities for work in this field are still lacking. The tendency to ascribe this lack of concern to lack of interest on the part of the students still persists. It appears that professional schools, and the professions as a whole, have, in too many instances, abandoned their responsibility for leadership and have been content merely to reflect the slow development of interest on the part of the community.

Fortunately, there are signs of developing interest in some of the schools, which augurs well for the future of social work with this particular group. There are indications of a growing appreciation of the concept of old age as being part of the total life cycle and of the sanctity of human life, no matter what the age of the person may be. This aroused interest, together with the increase of elderly in our society, the pressure of their problems, and their growing ability to voice their demands for attention to their numerous needs, which have resulted in ever more adequate services, will have the same impact on professional schools and will influence the training of future generations of social workers.

Need for Research

Our discussion has demonstrated that the hypothesis which was posed at the beginning has been proved to be correct, namely, that the process of aging imposes changes and losses on the individual in all areas of living and that these changes have a significant impact on the family relationships between the older and the younger generations.

We have seen that the changes which occurred in our society and the pressures exerted by the increased number of elderly people in our midst have had a visible effect on our attitude toward them. The indifference and neglect of earlier years are slowly giving way to a concern for the older person's welfare, and to an appreciation of the need to help solve such difficulties as they encounter.

Progress, however, continues to be slow. Such measures as have been undertaken, have been focused on specific needs as these became particularly stressful from time to time. This piecemeal approach has, until recently, blinded us to the fact that the difficulties encountered by the elderly are interrelated and that they affect and aggravate each other. We are only now beginning to recognize that economic insufficiency, for instance, has a deleterious effect on health, while persistent ill-health often leads to a depletion of financial resources. Both lack of funds and ill-health may necessitate changes in living arrangements, disrupting the individual's accustomed way of life. The loss of a mate or of contemporaries may result in loneliness and isolation, which can impair the individual's physical and mental health, and so on in a vicious circle. An understanding of this interrelationship and its effects will go a long way to insure more adequate planning.

An important factor which has stood in the way of our inability to meet the needs of the elderly is our lack of reliable information as to what the elderly require and what can and must be done to meet such needs. Most important is our lack of knowledge of what the elderly want for themselves. Such studies as are available are too often based on scanty data. One cannot escape the impression that the contradictory conclusion so frequently encountered are strongly tainted by the authors' personal biases. As was said by Justice Benjamin N. Cardozo many years ago: "We may try to see things as objectively as we please. None the less, we can never see them with any eyes except our own."

As an example of such contradictory conclusions, one may cite studies which claim that family members take care of their elderly relatives, while others maintain that the elderly are being neglected by the younger members of the family group. Undoubtedly, there are instances of both these attitudes, but we do not really know how frequently one or the other prevails. Nor do we have reliable information as to the factors which determine these attitudes.

Similarly, when we discuss "meaningful roles" for the elderly, we appear to assume that certain roles are meaningful to them, but we do not really know what the elderly themselves consider meaningful. Perhaps what has value for one may not have value for another. In this, as in a great many other situations, they are no different from the rest of us.

Furthermore, in a discussion of the needs and the attitudes of the elderly, there appears to be a lack of definition of terms. For instance, there has been considerable discussion as to whether or not the elderly are an isolated group. We do not know what the term "isolation" means to the particular discussant, for it is apparent that the different authors do not mean the same thing, nor do we know what the alleged isolation means to the older person.

As was so aptly pointed out:

It is true enough that any of us might contrive the story of any elderly person's life. . . . We could manufacture suppositions about what he is experiencing . . . how he regards the past . . . how he views the future, and all the rest. . . . It is so easy to suppose that he feels the way we think we would feel if we were in his situation, or simply that he must feel the way we think it proper for an elderly person to feel. . . . We do this sort of thing much of the time, without realizing that what we are hearing is not his story, but merely the sound of our own voices.[21]

It would appear that in order to plan intelligently for the elderly, we must secure reliable answers to these and other questions through properly controlled research. The results of such research would give us a better understanding of the aged, of their actual needs, their attitudes, their desires. It would lead to innovative techniques, based on more accurate

[21] Kastenbaum, p. 126.

knowledge than we now possess, and these techniques would enable us to deal more effectively with the older person, whether through casework or group work. The findings of such research could become an important part of a system of values to be pursued through appropriate action.

We are still a long way from being in a position to undertake such thoroughgoing research. Authorities still disagree as to whether there is real value in a prolonged life span. At a conference on "Extension of Human Life Span" held at the Center for the Study of Democratic Institutions at Santa Barbara, California, it was claimed on the one hand that

there is little evidence that society can make available the money, personnel, energy, and skills required to meet their [aged persons'] needs. . . . For maximum social benefit and minimum social harm, it might be wise to postpone extension of the human life-span until balancing social changes are achieved. . . . If we decrease the length of senescence by advances in aging control, we may prolong tedium, drudgery, years of depression and anxiety.[22]

Another speaker pointed to the misconception of the statement that

a longer life-span will enormously increase the number of marginally functioning persons, create greater demand for medical care and services, housing, etc., and force us to allocate a greater part of our gross national product to this "unproductive, parasitic" sector of the population. Increased longevity cannot be attained without general improvement in adult health and functioning. . . . If senescence is postponed, then the attendant decreases in function will also be postponed, as will the social burdens they impose. Postponement of senescence would permit additional years of truly productive activity—almost doubling their (the workers') net lifetime contribution to the assets of society.[23]

[22] Goldfarb, pp. 5–6.   [23] Strehler, p. 9.

These opposing points of view give a striking illustration of our lack of knowledge and what is even more important, of the prevailing attitudes in our society as regards the elderly. What we can accept as a guide to future action for the welfare of the elderly, as well as of other segments of the population, is Dr. R. N. Butler's statement that "when we know more of the great themes of old age—death, time, change, grief, loneliness, despair—we shall be able to contribute to our understanding of the other periods in the brief changing life of man." [24]

Impact of Social Attitudes

Important as is reliable knowledge as a basis for future action on behalf of the elderly, the one factor which more than any other has stood in the way of adequate planning and purposeful activity is the attitude of society. There can be little question that in our youth-work-achievement-oriented society the elderly are regarded as worthless and not entitled to the respect usually accorded younger members. The elderly are seen as incompetent, incapable of handling either their physical requirements or their emotional needs. The contributions made by them during their working years are denigrated and disregarded. They are

expected to be content with half measures—discounts, tax concessions, reduced bus fares, or reduced admission to theaters, and charity from their children or charitable agencies. They have watched as the special needs of other segments of the population are rightfully understood and met, while their own needs

[24] Butler, p. 596.

for mobility, for increased socialization, for the sense of worth which comes from productive activity, go unheeded.[25]

This attitude is inculcated in the young, if not by precept, then by merely subjecting them to witnessing actual practice, and passed on from generation to generation with little thought of the effect of this attitude on their own future. We seem to forget that "disease, old age and death pursue all of us," as pointed out by Plato many years ago.

The medical profession provides a sampling of society as a whole in its attitude toward the elderly. Experience shows that too often the teachers of the young physicians do little to instill in the future practitioners the importance of the human being regardless of his age, or the need to provide the best possible care for him. It is reflected in the dearth of medical literature devoted primarily to the ailments of the older generation, or to the problems which confront them in that area.

The same attitude is seen in the thinking and action of other professional groups concerned with the problems of the aged and is reflected in the inadequate provisions for meeting their needs.

In the last analysis, necessary changes in the condition of the elderly will depend on the changes in society's attitude to them. Not only the growing number of elderly people, but their growing ability to voice their needs and act on their own behalf will have its effect. There is ample evidence that the elderly are no longer content with remaining the "silent, underprivileged minority." They are beginning to organize and exert their influence. Take, for example, the

[25] Martin, Meeting of Montana Governor's Conference on Aging," p. 10.

American Association of Retired Persons, the Retired Teachers Association, and the National Council of Senior Citizens, as well as other groups on state and local levels. The programs outlined in the Older Americans Act and in the Six-point Program of New York State, previously referred to, are hopeful indications of future developments.

There is growing understanding that the needs of the elderly can be met most effectively through legislative action, and the elderly themselves are taking steps to exercise their voting power to that end. Candidates for office are beginning to realize that the elderly represent a group which must be taken into consideration by them.

The effect of this voting power is beginning to be seen in the discussions of the need to insure better economic help and more adequate medical care. These efforts will serve to liberate the elderly from the necessity of depending on the younger generation—a dependence which is damaging to both the old and the young—and would remove a source of the irritation and unhappiness so detrimental to family harmony.

Much more, however, needs to be done if the status and image of the older person are to be altered, and his worth and dignity to be considered as important as the worth and dignity of the younger person. In this, as in many other situations, it is difficult to devise a single, clear-cut answer as to how the goal is to be achieved. Here we are confronted with the problem that not only do the needs differ from individual to individual, but they differ also among the age groups within the period designated as "old age."

For the younger among this group, it is important that they be helped to overcome the apathy and depression which so often assail them, by giving them an opportunity to demonstrate their continued capability of contributing to society. Beginnings toward this end have been made, and it is hoped that more will be done in the future. We must capitalize on our acquired knowledge that the elderly respond positively to any opportunity to utilize their skill and experience, as well as to the prospect of learning and growing.

The achievement of such an important role in life has a bearing not only on the way the older person regards himself, but also on the way in which he is regarded by the younger generation. The useful older person cannot be regarded as being no longer part of life. The appreciation of what the elderly can do, makes it possible for the younger to see and admire those qualities which have contributed so much to their own prosperity and the advances enjoyed by them.

It is understandable that not all the elderly can continue to contribute. Increasing disabilities, brought on so often as the years advance, may interfere with the older person's ability to meet his needs unaided. The availability of aids, previously discussed, helps to relieve the burden imposed on family members. They can remain free to supply the warmth and concern which are so important to the elderly and which can make it possible for the elderly to remain part of their families, avoiding institutionalization which is fraught with so much stress and pain.

In order to safeguard the integrity of the family and strengthen family ties, it is important that the young be inculcated at an early age with the understanding that illness and disabilities do not detract from the value and dignity of the old, but that they make them particularly vulnerable, in need of even more attention and love and of the knowledge that their predicament is understood. Such lessons learned in youth are not easily forgotten.

242 LOOKING TO THE FUTURE

We are still a long way from realizing the full impact of the older person's deprivations and the services needed to compensate them in some small measure for such deprivations. We must acquire an understanding of society's attitude toward age and the aging, and of the relationships that exist between age groups, to a much greater extent than we now possess. Only full recognition of the importance which these forces have on the welfare of the elderly and on the unity of the family will enable us eventually to provide the help which is so badly needed.

To summarize the difficulties under which the elderly labor, as well as what can and cannot be done to help, one can do no better than quote from a paper presented by Clark Tibbits at the Annual Conference on Aging at the University of Michigan in 1965:

The middle and later years, as perhaps no other stage of life, are characterized by an almost infinite variety of threats to emotional stability and efficiency, to ego identity and integration, and to the ability to see the world realistically and to maintain oneself in equilibrium with it.

In discussing what can be done, Mr. Tibbits concludes:

Virtually every aspect of living is involved in maintaining mental health and efforts to maintain it must be broad ranging. . . . It is obvious that some of these threats or insults, such as reduced income and lack of a positive defined place in society, are unnecessary; that some, such as isolation and the effects of certain illnesses, can be mitigated; and that some, such as biological decline and social change, are inevitable and that the individual, with the backing of society, must reorganize his self-concepts and behavior on the basis of the limitations they impose.[26]

He points out that "the promotion and preservation of mental health presupposes a good deal of social intervention,

[26] Tibbits, p. 3.

changes in social values, and remaking of the environment of middle-aged and older people." [27]

This statement presents us with a platform of effective and essential action if the status of the elderly is to be improved.

[27] *Ibid.*, p. 4.

REFERENCES

Beck, L. Clagett, M.D., and Esther K. Stangle. "Geriatric Rehabilitation," *Geriatrics*, July, 1968, pp. 118–26.

"Benefits of Planning in Pre-retirement Years," *Geriatrics*, March, 1969. p. 50.

Bishop, M. W., and M. J. Manby. "Social Needs of the Elderly," *British Hospital Journal and Social Service Review.* September, 1969, p. 1710.

Blenkner, Margaret. "Social Work and Family Relationships in Later Years with Some Thoughts on Filial Maturity," in *Social Structure and the Family Generational Relations*, ed. Ethel Shanas and Gordon F. Streib. Englewood Cliffs, N.J.: Prentice-Hall, 1965.

Bluestone, E. M., M.D. "Medical Social Service—a Physician-Administrator's Confession of Faith," *Hospitals*, May 16, 1962, pp. 52–58.

—— "The Growing Impact of Longer Years on Society—a Salute to Youth and a Plea," in *Depth and Extent of the Geriatric Problem*, ed. Minna Field. Springfield, Ill.: Charles C. Thomas, 1970.

Brisette, Gerard G. *The Significance of Life-Goals in Aging Adjustment—a Pilot Study.* Research Monograph No. 9, California Department of Mental Hygiene, 1967.

Bromley, D. R. *Psychology of Human Aging.* Baltimore, Md.: Penguin Books, 1966.

Brotman, Herman B. "Who Are the Aged: a Demographic View." Unpublished monograph, 1968.

—— *Every Tenth American.* Supplement to the Institute of Gerontology Bulletin *Adding Life to Years*, XV, No. 10 (1968) 3.

Butler, R. N. "Research and Clinical Observations on the Psychologic Reactions in Physical Changes with Age," in Mayo Clinic *Proceedings*, No. 2, 1967.

"A Center Takes Its Program to the People—with Results Above Expectations," *Aging*, June–July, 1969, pp. 6–7.

Chandler, Susannah. "A Comprehensive Program for the Elderly in Rural Areas." Mimeographed. New York: National Council on Aging, Inc.; no date.

Coe, Rodney M., *et al.* "The Response to Medicare," *Public Health Reports*, LXXXIII, No. 4 (1968), 271–76.

Cohen, Wilbur J. "Action Line for Aging," *Aging*, December, 1968, p. 17.

"Community Service Society Dropping Casework to Give Aid to Slum Groups," New York *Times*, January 29, 1971, pp. 15 and 46.

Cowen, Emory L., *et al.* "Utilization of Retired People as Mental Health Aides with Children," *American Journal of Orthopsychiatry*, XXXVIII (1968), 900–909.   ,

Cummings, E., and William E. Henry. *Growing Old*. New York: Basic Books, 1961.

Drake Preretirement Center Conducts National Survey. Supplement to the Institute of Gerontology Bulletin *Adding Life to Years*, XVII, No. 4 (1970), 7.

Droller, Hugo, M.D. "Does Community Care Really Reach the Elderly Sick?" *Gerontologia Clinica*, 1969, pp. 170–82.

—— *Institutionalisation. Interdiscipl. Topics Gerontol.*, III (1969), 103–10.

Ewald, William R. "Great Cohort of Retired Persons May Inaugurate Shift from a Work- to a Leisure-oriented Society," *Geriatric Focus*, IX, No. 7 (1970), 2–3.

Federal Government to Use Drake Preretirement Manual. Supplement to the Institute of Gerontology Bulletin *Adding Life to Years*, XVII, No. 4 (1970), 7.

"First Annual Report on Medicare," Washington, D.C., 90th Congress, Second Session, House Document No. 331, June, 1968, pp. 3–13.

Folsom, James C., M.D. "Kind Firmness Therapy in Aged Depression," *Geriatric Focus*, VIII, No. 13 (1969), 1–5.

Fowler, Floyd J., Jr., and Mary Ellen McCalla. "Correlates of High Morale in Community-based Aged," *Geriatric Focus*, VIII, No. 18 (1968), 1–5.

Friedman, Sigmund L., and M. Ann Coleman. "Evaluation of Medical Facilities in Institutions for the Aged," in *Depth and Extent of the*

Geriatric Problem, ed. Minna Field. Springfield, Ill.: Charles V. Thomas, 1970.

Gelber, Beatrice. "A Pilot Study of Retired Scientists." Unpublished monograph, Grant 1 RO3 MH 16253-01 from the National Institute of Mental Health, Fort Lauderdale, Fla., 1969.

Goldfarb, Alvin A., M.D. "Harmful Psychological Effects of Increased Life Expectancy," *Geriatric Focus*, IX, No. 6 (1970), 5–6.

Gosette, Helen M. *The Rationale for Adoption of Social Work in Nursing Homes*. Supplement to the Institute of Gerontology Bulletin *Adding Life to Years*, XVI, No. 3 (1969), 1–4.

Hirsh, Hyman. "Back-to-School Programs for Retired Professionals," *Geriatrics*, January, 1969, pp. 36–41.

Hoffman, Frederick. "The Problem of Poverty and Pensions in Old Age," in *Proceedings of the National Conference of Charities and Corrections, 1908*. Fort Wayne, Ind.: Fort Wayne Printing Co., 1908.

"Independence for the Aged," *British Hospital Journal and Social Service Review*, May, 1969, p. 1014.

Kastenbaum, Robert. "The Foreshortened Life Perspective," *Geriatrics*, August, 1969, pp. 126–34.

Klein, Wilma, *et al. Promoting Mental Health of Older People through Group Methods*. New York: Mental Health Materials Center, 1965.

Knowles, John, M.D. "Medicare, Medicaid Reforms Urged by Advisory Committee, *Geriatrics*, September, 1969, pp. 26–31.

Leake, Chauncey D. "Attitudes of Medical Students toward Aged," *Geriatrics*, July, 1969, pp. 58–59.

Ledgerwood, Ian. "Report on Retirement Cities," *Modern Maturity*, August–September, 1969, pp. 21–23.

Margulec, I., M.D. "Two Decades of Caring for Aged in Israel," in *Depth and Extent of the Geriatric Problem*, ed. Minna Field. Springfield, Ill.: Charles C. Thomas, 1970.

Martin, Alexander Reid, M.D., and Ralph Slater, M.D. "The Creative Use of Free Time," in *Depth and Extent of the Geriatric Problem*, ed. Minna Field. Springfield, Ill.: Charles C. Thomas, 1970.

Martin, John B. "Meeting of Montana's Governor's Conference on Aging," *Aging*, December, 1969, p. 10.

—— "New Commissioner on Aging Gives Priority to Health, Housing, Jobs," *Geriatrics*, July, 1969, pp. 26–37.

"Mature Temps' Birthday Promise," *Modern Maturity*, April–May, 1970, p. 65.

Mobility of the Population of the United States, April, 1958 to 1959. Current Population Reports, Population Characteristics. Washington, D.C.: U.S. Department of Commerce, 1960. Series P20, No. 104, p. 15.

"Multiphasic Screening Procedures Stressed in Federal Health Programs," *Geriatrics,* January, 1969, pp. 30–34.

"Nash Cites 'Penny Pinching' by H.E.W., Neglect in Programs," *AARP News Bulletin,* II, No. 7 (1970), 1 and 4.

Neugarten, Bernice L. "Dynamics of Transitions of Middle Age to Old Age," *Geriatric Focus,* January, 1970, pp. 1–9.

Oberleder, M. "Crisis Therapy for the Mentally Ill Aged," *Geriatric Focus,* VIII, No. 9 (1969), 1–6.

Older Americans Act of 1965. "Declaration of Objectives for Older Americans." Public Law 89–73. 89th Congress, H.R. 3708, Title I, p. 1.

"Presidential Task Force on Aging Urges Action Now to Help Elderly," *Aging,* August, 1970, p. 45.

"Psychiatric Screening of Geriatric Patients," *Geriatric Focus,* VIII, No. 12 (1969), 3.

Rubinow, I. M., M.D. *Social Insurance.* New York: Henry Holt & Co., 1916.

—— *Quest for Security.* New York: Henry Holt & Co., 1934.

Shanas, Ethel, *et al. Old People in Three Industrial Societies.* New York: Allerton Press, 1968.

"6-Point Program Urged in New York State for Dependent Aging," *Aging,* December, 1969, p. 16.

"65+ Medical Costs $590; 21% Rise: Non-elderly Bill $195, Up 10%," *Aging,* December, 1969, p. 12.

"Social Work Team with Aging Family Service Clients." Second Summary Progress Report to the National Institute of Mental Health by Family Service Association of America. Unpublished monograph, 1968.

Sprague, Norman. "Testimony on the 1967 Amendments to the Social Security Act before the Senate Committee on Finance." Unpublished document, 1967.

Srole, Leo. "Progress Report on Geel Foster Family Care Research Project." Unpublished monograph, 1970.

Strehler, Bernard, M.D. "10 Myths that Obstruct Basic Research in Aging," *Geriatric Focus,* IX, No. 6 (1970), 1–10.

Talmer, Margot, and Bernard Kutner. "Disengagement and the Stress of Aging," *Journal of Gerontology,* XXIV, No. 1 (1969), 70–75.

Tibbitts, Clark. "Societal Provisions for Maintaining Mental Health of the Older Population." Unpublished manuscript, 1965.

"U.S. 1970 Census of Population Advance Report." General Population Statistics, February, 1971, Table II, p. 4.

"Visit to the 500-year-old Prototype of the Therapeutic Community," *Geriatric Focus*, VII, No. 19 (1968), 2–3.

"Voting and Registration in Elections of 1968." Current Population Characteristics, Census Bureau, U.S. Department of Commerce, December, 1969, p. 20.

"White House Conference Urges Nutritional Aids for the Elderly," *Aging*, February–March, 1970, p. 19.

INDEX